ALSO BY DONALD S. CONNERY:
THE SCANDINAVIANS
THE IRISH

ONE
AMERICAN
TOWN

DONALD S. CONNERY

SIMON AND SCHUSTER • NEW YORK

FOR MY CHILDREN—AND YOURS

In the loveliest town of all, where the houses were white and high and the elm trees were green and higher than the houses, where the front yards were wide and pleasant and the back yards were bushy and worth finding out about, where the streets sloped down to the stream and the stream flowed quietly under the bridge, where the lawns ended in orchards and the orchards ended in fields and the fields ended in pastures and the pastures climbed the hill and disappeared over the top toward the wonderful wide sky, in this loveliest of all towns Stuart stopped to get a drink of sarsaparilla.

E. B. WHITE, Stuart Little

I have no doubt myself that one of the great unspoken forces in the life of Americans today is a longing for community, for human contact and human concern. People feel themselves in the grip of institutions whose values are inhuman, a juggernaut that sweeps them along with no one to hear their cry. Why does that feeling exist? What makes America so uncommunal, so lonely a country?

ANTHONY LEWIS

SNAPSHOT

OUR TOWN is an early-rising town. The farmers are out with the cows by the time the mothers of school-age children wake up to get breakfast at six or so. The teen-agers, who face a long ride up the river valley to the regional high school, catch the first of the yellow school buses that grind up and down the hills. The morning sun glistens on the dew-damp meadows. Some husbands drive off to distant offices and factories. The carpenters and plumbers gather up their tools. A teacher bicycles to class. Traffic picks up. A truck rolls into the lumberyard on Main Street. The shopkeepers open their doors. The town goes about its business: building, producing, plowing, teaching, selling, shopping, fixing, cleaning, keeping things going. Mail is delivered. Newspapers are picked up at the Milk Bar. The state trooper makes his rounds. Senior citizens meet for coffee in the library. The once-a-day bus comes by, heading north. The fire siren announces noon. A pause for lunch. The town character rocks for a while in front of the antique shop. The day wears on. The daily freight train rumbles across the highway. The bank closes at three as the children journey home. Visits to the doctor. Baseball played at the edge of a cornfield. A canoe glides on the river. The sounds of lawn mowers, piano practice and small talk in front of the funeral home. The First Selectman closes his office and goes up to the lake. Soon after five the lady in the post office comes out and hauls down the flag. The stores lock up. The pharmacy and the filling stations stay open awhile longer. The church steeple catches the last rays of the afternoon sun. At six the bells of the boarding school ring across the valley. People wash up, eat, watch the news on television. After supper the Board of Finance meets in the town hall. Volunteer firemen play cards in the firehouse. The preacher writes his Sunday sermon. Children do their homework. Only an occasional car passes through town, headlights dimmed by the late evening fog. A young couple returns from the movie house in the next town. The package store's neon sign turns itself off. By midnight the village is well asleep. Moonlight bathes the darkened houses on the hillsides. Crickets and bullfrogs claim the night.

INTRODUCTION

IN HIS PLAY *Our Town*, first performed in 1938, Thornton Wilder described the everyday goings-on of a place he called Grover's Corners, New Hampshire, population 2,642, as it was in 1901 and in the early years of this century.

As the play unfolds, the stage manager mentions that one of the more noteworthy happenings in town is the construction of a new bank building. "And they've asked a friend of mine what they should put in the cornerstone for people to dig up," he says, far in the future. "So I'm going to have a copy of this play put in the cornerstone and the people a thousand years from now'll know a few simple facts about us . . . the way we were: in our growing up and in our marrying and in our living and in our dying."

Many years after *Our Town* had become established as an American classic, Wilder explained that the play was not offered simply as a picture of life in a New Hampshire village. Rather, "It is an attempt to find a value above all price for the smallest events in our daily life. I have made the claim as preposterous as possible, for I have set the village against the largest dimensions of time and place."

Wilder's "preposterous" claim occurs to me now as I proceed to put on the record some things about the place where I now live: one small town in the northeast corner of America at the beginning of the eighth decade of the twentieth century. Unlike Grover's Corners, this is a real town, full (or not so full) of real people. Like Grover's Corners, it is mostly just "a nice place to live." It is one of many hundreds of pleasant but easily overlooked settlements tucked away in the hills and valleys of rural New England. It is one of many thousands of versions of Hometown, U.S.A. When set against the 200 million and more inhabitants of these 50 American states or the billions of people on this small pebble in the universe, ours is a most insignificant community. We are a few grains of sand on a vast human beach. You will never see us in the headlines or on the television news. "Nothing happens here," as they say, though not long ago strangers came up the mountain and shot two of my neighbor's pet llamas. And every so often at town meeting we get worked up over such controversial things as the new sewer and the cost of snow removal.

Although we have in our township more square miles than Manhattan or the island of Hong Kong, we number only 2,000 people, or something like 800 families. We are greatly outnumbered by four-footed creatures: deer, cattle, sheep, horses, donkeys, goats, pigs, dogs, cats, raccoons, skunks, porcupines, beavers, squirrels, moles, llamas and one shaggy yak.

We have plenty of elbow room, and that helps explain why we get along pretty well with one another. Four thousand of our 25,000 acres are set aside as state parks, nature preserves and other public lands. We even have a fair-sized Indian reservation, which only yesterday lost its last Indian. We occupy less than nine pages of a small telephone book that we share with six other towns. We account for only one one-thousandth of one percent of the American people.

More to the point, ours is a reasonably happy and contented community, snug in the country greenery, and as such we would appear to have little to do with the cataclysmic issues and fearful anxieties of the age. Naturally enough, though not altogether to our credit, we worry more about the school budget and where to put the town dump than about foreign affairs or civil rights or the woes of the cities and suburbs where most of our fellow Americans live.

At a time of exploding population and abuse of the environment, we have the same number of people in our village and in the surrounding hills as we had a century and a half ago, and we have far less pollution than in the ironworking days of the 1800s. In an age when men live in the mass in high-pressure technological societies, we are spared the daily tensions of traffic jams and rush-hour crowds. We only occasionally hear an airplane—though snowmobiles are beginning to be a nuisance in the winter. We never ride in an elevator or a subway unless we have business to do in the city. Many of us walk to work and go home for lunch. Some, like myself, work at home, and we can go for weeks without ever putting on a tie. Like rural people everywhere, we can always find time for a chat. New York and other cities are only a few hours away by car, and we pick up their television signals, but our air is clear, our water is clean, and when I wake up with the sun I can often see deer standing beneath the apple trees. We rarely experience any serious violence. Only the old-timers can recall when the last murder was done, and I have yet to see anyone strike a blow in anger, though I suppose it happens. There is a burglary now and then, usually the work of outsiders, but we become concerned about crime only when we are reminded that it is a grave national issue. Some of us never lock our doors.

All in all, in an era of upheaval when so much of American life seems to be out of joint, or spinning out of control, and when so many people feel like displaced persons in their own country, we go on pretty much as usual: changing slowly, going to church, sending the kids to school, talking about the weather (we have a lot of weather to talk about), getting our work done, enjoying life. Our little local newspaper is aptly named *The Good Times Dispatch.*

And so I must ask myself why I think this single small, stable community is worth my writing about and your reading about. There are, God knows, far more crucial and momentous subjects to engage our attention. Although this is one of those American places that a Tom Sawyer or a Grandma Moses would find agreeable, I have no interest in contributing to the nostalgic or escapist impulses of a nation in crisis and certainly no desire to encourage any complacent notion that things in America are not as bad as they seem. I would argue, in fact, that things are worse than they seem and that this fractured and demoralized society is in desperate need of some form of humanist revolution. Believing this, yet choosing to settle in the snug corner of a healthy little town, as if in another country, raises uncomfortable questions of personal conscience.

Although some time has gone by and we are well dug in, I am still a newcomer here, a "city fellow" come to live in one of the town's fine old farmhouses, several serpentine miles up Skiff Mountain, after many years of professional wandering about America and foreign parts. I have been a journalist all my working life, an observer of the human condition on five continents. It is hardly surprising that I should have returned to my deeply troubled native land with an acute sense of foreboding about the future. I have seen too much of the world to be able to escape the knowledge that man, the most ingenious creature of all, is in the process of ensuring his own extinction—and with unseemly haste.

Thornton Wilder spoke of men "a thousand years from now" digging up the cornerstone of the Grover's Corners bank building and finding some artifacts of our age. Today there are eminent scientists and scholars who question whether the human species will make it to the year 2000, now less than 30 years away. Even the most incurable optimist, who can ignore the several specters that haunt the world, is bound to admit that a great many of the good things of life—including the most commonplace civilities—seem to be slipping through our fingers.

It has become a cliché to speak of the dehumanization of modern man and of the demeaning and even maddening pressures of urbanized, industrialized society. America the Beautiful becomes increasingly ugly, and the American Dream is part nightmare. Never in history have a people created so much so fast and destroyed so much in the process. Our greed and violence, the way we have ravaged nature, the rank inequities and injustices of a society screaming for renewal—they are as obvious as the ghettos and polluted rivers and wasted lives.

Not long ago an elderly farmer in the Berkshire hills of Massachusetts explained to a visiting writer that "when you talk about the past you're talking about folks that loved the future. They came here in the 1700s and 1800s, when this was nothing but woods. They cleared the land, walled up, planted trees, built to last and made a fine future for those who came after. The church, the school, the family—those three things had to be. Today, their skills are forgotten, their ideas don't count. All gone."

All gone?

Not quite. Their ideas and even some of their skills still count for something in this small town at least, however modern-minded we may be, however far we are from being simple, pious rustics. And the church, the school, the family—they are here too, as real and as enduring as our great trees and old stone walls. I cannot say for sure that the townspeople love the future, but they do not seem to be in much fear of it.

What am I to make of all this? Is ours simply an extraordinarily fortunate place that has managed to escape the worst ravages of what some people call progress? And if that be the case, are we anything more than an outdoor museum, an isolated patch of green on a concrete landscape?

We are fortunate, all right, but not so extraordinary as one might think. If someone were to work up a proper definition of the Good Life, or be able to measure the gross national quality as neatly as the gross national product, our town would surely earn high marks—but only as one of many. For there are still, in this rich and varied and not yet ruined country, a multitude of distinctive and delightful hamlets, villages, river towns, mountain towns, prairie towns, leafy suburbs, amiable small cities and congenial big-city neighborhoods. They demonstrate that a genuinely civilized life on a human scale, however imperfect, still exists and is still possible in the U.S.A.

Beyond the headlines and the anger and the tumult of accelerating change, there remains an America of values, roots, loving families, peaceful pursuits, kindly ways. I have in mind all those harmonious and manageable communities where change is more steady than spectacular, where people cherish their easygoing style of life and the character of their surroundings. They are places of obvious integrity that have somehow managed to mature gracefully without being exploited, uprooted, paved over or left to die on the vine. Places that are therefore most vulnerable. One review of a recent novel about a New England village described it as the kind of town that is "so quiet and beautiful, it is bound to be spoiled."

Such communities are precious national resources, well worth preserving and fighting for. They are, of course, far from perfect. In fact, their human scale makes their human failings all too obvious. They include places that are doubtlessly too parochial and unexciting for anyone with a zest for life, though the American town has come a long way from the narrow-minded and culturally impoverished world of *Main Street*. They carry on a style of life and a turn of mind that most Americans, I believe, still cherish and even idealize. I, for one, find it reassuring to have so close at hand so much evidence of individual self-reliance, self-confidence, good humor, good manners, concern for neighbors, readiness to lend a helping hand, pride in town and nation, and respect for the natural world.

There are even times when I can bring myself to believe that a town like this one, far from being a relic of the past, is something of a model for the future. Many Americans who live in the mass are questioning the tyranny of mindless technological change and are resisting the control over their lives of giant governmental and corporate bureaucracies. There is a visible yearning for a greater harmony of man and nature and for the intimacy of participation in a society of reasonable dimensions, whether a commune, a rural settlement, a New Town, an old town, or an aroused city neighborhood that has won for itself some measure of community control.

Speaking as one who has come to the village experience after having lived in cities as large as Tokyo, London, New York, New Delhi and Moscow, there is something almost intoxicating about knowing that your views and your vote count, and about seeing that you can make an immediate personal imprint on the conditions of your life. If nothing else, you become less cynical and despairing. You begin to believe in the possibility of a rejuvenation of your country, knowing at first hand that there is still enough of the best of America to build on. You can even imagine that an America restored to her full moral energies might inspire mankind to seek a more humane future.

When you live close to the top of a mountain, as I do, and have nothing in the way of your vision but green pastures, dark woods and gentle hills framed in golden sunsets, you are likely to have such lofty thoughts. Fortunately, there are always things to bring you down to earth. The water pipe to the barn has frozen. There is manure to be shoveled and other work to be done. The deacons are meeting in the parish house tonight. Another old-timer has died. The First Selectman has just become a father. They say in the village that the new school addition will be ready for the fall term. These are the things you feel most comfortable talking about. At a time in history when the continuity of life is profoundly threatened, they give you a sense of the durability of man on earth.

This book, then, is about such things. I am making my own preposterous claim for the value of the everyday events of this one obscure community, knowing that they can be multiplied by the millions across the country. What knowledge I have of this town has come to me, just by living here, in bits and pieces: personal observation, scraps of conversation, stories in the local paper, sermons, gossip, recollections of natives, impressions of newcomers, old records and maps and photographs, skeletons buried in the Historical Society's files. And here and now I thank all those generous townspeople who have, wittingly and unwittingly, helped me understand something of the essence of our way of life.

Because I would like the reader to share this learning experience, I propose to guide him informally through four seasons of a year in the life of the town: taking things as they come, listening to the things people say and setting down some facts and reflections as if in a log or diary.

Please note that on the pages following I have put between quotation marks a scattering of comments about the town by people in the town. Being respectful of their privacy and personal feelings, however, I do not say who said what. Nor do I probe into private lives, though I mention our quirks and problems and passions. It is the personality of the community as a whole which concerns me the most. If I neglect to mention the name of the town, it is only because I am concerned about the effects of overexposure. I have come to care deeply about the survival of this one small place—and of all others like it. They are an endangered species.

SPRING

THE SHADOW of the long winter is lifting. When I go out to the barn in the morning to feed the horses, soon after six o'clock, the sun is already up and about. Not too many weeks ago I had to find my way in the dark, stumbling in high boots through fresh drifts of snow and fumbling for the light switch. We are now far into March. Spring has officially arrived, yet the meadows still lie under thick white blankets, and the leafless trees look fragile and forlorn as they lean away from the cold wind. The lakes and ponds are still frozen, but the ice went out quietly on the river on March 12, one of the earliest "ice outs" on record. According to the paper, "the person seen floating southbound on an ice floe Sunday reached safety, as there are no reports of missing persons."

On Main Street, conversations dwell on the imminence of spring weather, as if talking will hurry it up. We are afflicted by a kind of late-winter weariness now that the pleasures of skiing and skating have palled. Our nerves are a little on edge. Like our frozen streams and faucets, we need to be thawed out. The selectmen, worrying about the town's finances, are hoping that we will not be struck by another snowstorm that would cost us more money in road-clearing expenses. March is a grumpy month, too unpredictable to figure, but at least we know that April comes next, and then May, and soon summer.

• • •

In my childhood days life was different, in many ways, we were slower, still we had a good and happy life, I think, people enjoyed life more in their way, at least they seemed to be happier, they don't take time to be happy nowadays.

GRANDMA MOSES

• • •

The town is in the far green hills of Connecticut. It is one of the 169 townships that make a political map of the state look like a crudely done crazy quilt. Of the 169 ours is 13th in size but 148th in population and 160th in population density. According to our latest Grand List of taxable properties, we have in this settlement of 2,000 souls exactly 802 houses, 1,076 barns and other outbuildings, three small factories, 293 buildings for business, commercial and trading purposes, 1,445 motor vehicles, 142 horses, asses and mules, 480 cattle, 34 sheep and goats and 31 swine.

We also have a town hall and a Community House, a public elementary school and two private preparatory schools, a firehouse and a public library, one funeral home, one barber shop, two traffic lights, two post offices, two branch banks (under the same roof), three churches (plus two prep school chapels), three lakes (and half a dozen large ponds), four state parks and forests, eight summer camps, eight cemeteries, 62 miles of roads, 345 dogs, 440 schoolchildren, 1,111 registered voters, an annual budget of nearly $700,000 and a Grand List of more than $12 million.

Main Street is 397 feet above sea level. Mauwee Peak, the highest point in town, is 1,406 feet. Skiff Mountain: 1,350 feet.

Six people are licensed to keep bees.

• • •

The town has a somewhat homespun coat of arms, which can be seen not only on the sign welcoming visitors to the village but above the door of the Community House, on the lectern at town meetings and on the cover of the annual reports. It neatly sums up our history by means of an arrowhead, crown, cow, iron furnace, church, school and wheel of industry. It says the town was settled in 1720 and incorporated in 1739, half a century before the adoption of the United States Constitution. The artist got it a bit wrong, however. We were first settled in 1738. No one has ever bothered to make the correction.

. . .

Item in the paper. The town has just borrowed one million dollars. The purpose is to cover anticipated costs for our sewer and school-addition projects. It somehow makes us a bigger small town than we like to think we are. At the beginning of the century the entire cost of local government was less than $10,000, about a quarter of what it now costs us to transport the children to school. In 1892 the selectmen spent $38.50 on watering troughs.

. . .

James Gould Cozzens lived here once, went to school here and described the town ("New Winton") in a novel published in 1933. Times were hard nearly 40 years ago. The population had thinned out considerably, almost all the roads were unpaved and life in the hills above the valley was rough going, especially at times of deep snow and immobilizing mud.

. . .

In bad weather, or in winter, few cars attempted the climb to Cold Hill. It would be absolutely impossible for the school buses, so Cold Hill continued to have its small, shabby, one-room school for the children of the families living in the dozen poor farms which succeeded each other along the cleared strip of barren upland. No one of any means or influence lived on these drearily wind-swept acres, fifteen hundred feet, every foot difficult, above New Winton in the valley, so there was no reason for New Winton to add the great expense of making the road passable to its already sufficient trouble with roads.

JAMES GOULD COZZENS, *The Last Adam*

. . .

"When I grew up here in the 1930s this was an isolated farming community: dirt roads everywhere, a lot of farmers, lots of cattle. Not much money around. I remember a certain lady up on Skiff Mountain who would come to the valley every morning in her horse and wagon, carrying milk, and then she'd drive up again. Sometimes I would ride up with her and come down with the mailman, just for a lark."

• • •

"Older people in town ask me how I like living here. When I say that it's fine, that I really like it, they shake their heads and say that it isn't the way it used to be. They used to know everyone by sight, but now they say they see so many faces on the street they don't know. But my view is entirely different. After living in the city and in bigger towns, it's really fantastic to go down the street and recognize half the people you see."

• • •

"I prefer this way of life. I like my work. I have a garden. I walk a lot in the woods. I just enjoy the surroundings, the pace of life here. The smallness of a small town doesn't bother me; you know, the pettiness, the things people say about you. I'm just amused. But a lot depends on what you *do* here. If you're a businessman, a banker, some kind of professional, and have been used to doing things on a big scale, very efficiently, you might find there's nothing duller than working in a small town."

• • •

Easter Sunday. A snowstorm blows into town even though the frost is out of the ground. March left like a lamb and April has come in like a lion. Half a foot of snow covers land that was finally showing bare earth and even crocuses after the long winter siege. While Canadian geese rest on the ponds and flocks of ducks settle on the cold river, the snowplows are out on the roads, and the cross-country skiers are having their last fling of the season.

Few people were able to make it to the sunrise service on Spooner Hill.

• • •

We discovered, after moving into this neck of the New England woods, that there is nothing bland or undefined about the seasons. Each makes its special music and glows with colors of its very own. Spring is a life-giving time of green growth and flashing water. Summer is hot, lush, languid, but the nights can be refreshingly cool. Fall comes on crisp as newly minted money, and the trees rain golden leaves. Winter is as winter should be: ice and snow and long nights, reducing the life of the town to fundamentals. We hibernate during the cold months, just the basic townspeople. The midyear months of long hot days and balmy nights bring up from the city the weekenders and summer people, the campers and tourists, until the population doubles without our fully realizing it. When they finally drift away with the approach of winter, we become most like ourselves again: a trim ship of a town, battened down against the elements.

• • •

Township 1. In England, an ancient unit of administration identical in area with, or a division of, a parish *2.* In the United States, a primary unit of local government of varying character in different localities. In New England, where it is called *town*, it exists in its primitive form except as modified and partly subordinated by the later-formed units, the county and the state. In the northwestern states the county is the older unit and the township is a division of the county. In the southern states, the county is generally the more important unit, and townships, where they exist, are mere local divisions.

Webster's New Collegiate Dictionary

• • •

Because of the irregular shape of these townships, we share a common border with six other towns. Three of them have considerably fewer inhabitants than we have. Only 820 people, in one case. Our town is about six miles wide and eight miles north

to south. The official figure is 48 and a half square miles, easy for
the children to remember because our own portion is 48 and a
half acres, "more or less" (as the deed says) of farmhouse, barn,
fences, lawns, meadows, pastures and woods. The stream running
through this piece of land, three and a half miles up Skiff Mountain, connects to a brook that meets another brook that flows
down to the river. The river passes through the township like a
deep crease in a strong and calloused hand, and its presence is an
important fact in the life of the townspeople. It is not a big
enough river, this far up in the state, to do much for us econom-
ically, and so we have been spared the unsightly industrial growth
of more important river towns. It probably does us immeasurable
good spiritually, just by offering us a daily visual feast of sparkling waters and by giving us a sense of being linked, up and
down the long valley, to northern mountains and southern seas.

•　•　•

The Indians called the valley "the place beyond the mountains." One of the earliest white men to come this way, in 1694,
reported that it was "a hideous, howling wilderness." The first
settlers did not move in until 44 years later, but they soon made
it a thriving town.

•　•　•

"This was still frontier territory at that time. They auctioned
off the town to the highest bidders. They divided it into lots and
sections, beginning on the east side of the river. But the pioneers
didn't take long getting up your mountain because there's a kind
of plateau up there that's quite desirable farmland."

•　•　•

At the settlement of the town there was very little wood or timber of
any kind. The Indian practice of burning up the country had prevailed
to a great extent and most of the lands being dry and hilly were thus
prevented from being clothed with timber. Since a stop has been put
to this practice the hills and uncultivated grounds are well covered
with oak, walnut, chestnut, maple, ash, butternut, basswood and other

kinds of wood. Wherever lands have been cut over within a few years, the prevailing new growth is chestnut. The proportion of land unfit for cultivation is so great that were wood employed for no other use than for fuel, there would probably never be a scarcity. Yet within a few years the consumption by means of the forges for making iron has been so great that should it continue for some time longer, the scarcity will be great.

BARZILLAI SLOSSON, 1812

•   •   •

"Old Joel Pratt used to tell about going up on the hillsides where they burnt charcoal. There weren't any weeds. After the fire and so forth there'd be black ashes there, and he said he could raise a wagonload of tobacco on a charcoal pit. It was easy—just set it out and it growed, and he'd go in the fall and late summer and gather it in and bring it down."

•   •   •

"There have been four phases in the history of the town: the pioneer phase, the iron phase, the dairy-farming phase and now the What-is-it? phase. Sometimes you have to wonder how the town supports itself. I remember when the milk checks brought in most of our income. Now we've got a mixture of shops, little businesses, industry, education, farming, writers, artists, people raising horses and making money in different ways. But people with investments are carrying the town as well. We've got quite a few retired folks receiving income and doing their shopping in town. That helps keep things going."

•   •   •

Should the settlers of the eighteenth century or the farmers and ironworkers of the nineteenth century return to the town today they would have little trouble finding their way about, once they had grown accustomed to our paved roads, our peculiar means of transportation and the sight of so many trees on the once denuded land. Some things have hardly changed at all. A good many of the same houses and barns remain in use, and our hills are still marked with trails and dry stone walls laid out long ago. Our population is no greater than it was in the days when this was still a largely self-sufficient horse-and-wagon town deep in rural America.

The old maps are just about as up to date as the new maps. The old Schaghticoke Indian trail running alongside the twisting river is now our major thoroughfare, still only one lane in each direction and still snaking along as if today's driver had all the time in the world. Many of us like it that way and believe it saves us from being overwhelmed by so-called progress, but some people who use it every day take a different view. One schoolteacher calls it "a bicycle path" and "a contemptible substitute for a highway in the 1970s."

For much of the way through town the highway is paralleled by railroad tracks, but we see few trains these days. In the southwest corner of the town map—old or new—there is Bulls Bridge, one of the two bridges spanning the river as it flows through our territory and one of the last two covered bridges still in use in Connecticut. The other is in the next town just up the river.

Old Jacob Bull, after eight years' work, finished building the covered bridge in 1776, just in time for the Revolutionary War. Reasonably enough, he charged a toll for its use except of anyone going to church. Jacob's great-great-great-grandson runs the post office on Main Street and heads up our chamber of commerce. He also handles our funerals.

•   •   •

If you should die in this town in the winter when the ground is frozen we do not get around to burying you until spring. We keep the waiting dead in a vault behind the Episcopal church cemetery, across the road from Cliff's Garage.

•   •   •

The tree warden says that the road crew will soon be removing the dead elms along Spooner Hill, Bulls Bridge and Schaghticoke

Road. The wood will be burned to prevent the spread of Dutch elm disease. One by one, however, the century-old elms in all these towns are going. Along Main Street there are several huge trees bearing the yellow "C" of the condemned.

•   •   •

In the files of the Historical Society there is an old photograph of a white-bearded man wearing rough clothing and a doleful expression. He is identified as Thomas Leonard, 1784–1862, "the man who set all the trees from St. Andrew's Church to Bacon farm at ten cents per tree."

•   •   •

Although many places in rural America are having great difficulty getting or keeping adequate medical services, we are fortunate. There are good hospitals and clinics in adjoining towns, and we have two fine physicians of our own as well as three dentists and two visiting nurses. We also have a resident psychiatrist whose main office is in New York. The family dentist commutes from his horse farm in another state. Our physician is a young general practitioner, much involved in community affairs, who carries on the tradition of the old-time country doctor. He even makes house calls.

•   •   •

Law enforcement here is mainly the responsibility of a young state trooper who lives in town, works out of his patrol car and a town hall office and takes orders from the state police barracks half an hour upriver. We also have seven elected constables—four Republicans, three Democrats—whose authority is severely limited. Being a constable these days is more of an honor than a chore. In the years before the town acquired a resident trooper of its own, however, our most veteran constable was pretty much the lawman in charge. He is the first to admit, in his cheerful way, that the town was—and still is—so peaceful that he got to fire his gun only once in the line of duty in 47 years. He shot it out with a pair of post office robbers back in 1940. "One of their shots spun me around and knocked me flat," he relates, "and they got away. We never did catch up with them. I couldn't even make out their faces in the dark. But I saved the stamps."

•   •   •

Things have been going along smoothly in the town so far this year. This despite having to adjust ourselves to the retirement of our town clerk after 25 years in office ("She's the one who really runs the town"), of our fire chief after 15 years and of our assistant fire chief after 17 years.

The new year began with icy roads, great blasts of cold wind and some puzzlement over the big Christmas fire up at Spectacle Lake which destroyed the main building of our largest summer camp. It was "one of the most spectacular conflagrations" in the history of the town, according to the newspaper, yet it happened without anyone's noticing—which says something about the remoteness of some parts of the township. We all slept right through it.

Looking at events since Christmas, several grand old citizens have passed away, and seven babies were born. We went to the polls to approve a $475,000 sewer budget, and at a 17-minute town meeting we added $80,000 to our earlier budget of $780,000 for the new school addition. (Thanks to federal and state grants, the actual cost to the town will be $100,000 for the sewer and $430,000 for the school addition.) We had some emotional meetings about an outside developer's proposal to build a small ski area in the town. The Congregational church opened its new parish house. A few local teen-agers were arrested on narcotics charges, and the police chief of a neighboring town stopped by to give us a crash course in drug detection. There were a few raised eyebrows when he filled his pipe with marijuana and went puffing around the room to acquaint us with the smell.

•   •   •

"We have a remarkable assortment of backgrounds here: English, Irish, Polish, Alsatians, Swiss, and so on. Old Yankees mixed with European immigrants who came in during our iron age. Most are Protestants, divided between the Congregational and Episcopal churches, and perhaps 20 percent Catholics and a few Jews. It is hard to say. No one takes count, and going to church isn't the important thing it used to be."

* * *

"You know, it's really a great town. In the suburb where I used to live you would never have gone to a cocktail party and seen such a mixture of people as you get here—your grocer and garageman, the school principal, the retired farmer as well as artists and writers, young and old, all together. This is a very, very democratic place."

* * *

"I wish we could organize a spinsters' club of some kind. All the widows get together. The married couples get together. But the poor old spinsters just sit looking at each other."

* * *

"We have a lot of long-lived people in this town. It's one of the things that surprised the daylights out of me when I got here: the number of really old people, living on into their eighties and nineties."

* * *

It is a closely knit and congenial little town, but it has, of course, its cliques and personality clashes, its subterranean feuds and ancient antagonisms, its jealousies and misunderstandings. There are visible separations and groupings for reasons of age, money, education, occupation, pastimes or religious and political beliefs. Not that it matters much. There are beer drinkers and cocktail drinkers, horse riders and snowmobilers, card players and foreign-film fans, conservatives and liberals, old-timers and young upstarts, property owners and hired hands, mechanics and

academics, and so on, yet any of them might well share the same
church pew or see eye to eye at a budget hearing or town meeting. The farmer and the writer may have only a small acquaint-
ance, but their wives could be the friendliest of teaching col-
leagues at the grade school. There are so many overlapping social
circles and interest circles that the town functions with perhaps
as great a degree of harmony, and a minimum of abrasion, as
anyone could reasonably hope for. In fact, there is such a general air of reasonableness, at least in public, that some of the older
hands regret the passing of the days when there were cranky
characters about who were forever at each other's throat.

●   ●   ●

"It's silly to talk about divisions in the town—of this group as
against that group, or old-timers and newcomers—because there
are so many people here who get around and know everybody
and really care about everybody. They go out of their way to
get to know the new people. They talk to them in church, invite
them to parties. They're real bridge builders."

●   ●   ●

Inevitably, of course, there is a certain distance between the
natives and the newcomers. There are the basic townspeople:
those born and bred here, reinforced by those who have spent the
greater part of their lives in the town. And then there are the people who have moved in from elsewhere, particularly in the post-
World War II years of population expansion. Although the newcomers are now more numerous than the old families, it is the
latter who set the tone for the town. And this is something that
many new arrivals happily accept, for they consciously sought
out the ambiance of a settled New England village. Some families
have roots going back to the eighteenth century, and there are
mountains and roads named after them, but with one or two ex-
ceptions they have withdrawn from active leadership in local
government or business. The most influential families came to
town only a few generations ago. "Even so," one elderly resident

told me, "they are a little slow about accepting you as being part of the town. I came here as a young man and I've lived here all my life, but I'm not sure they've accepted me yet. Not, of course, that it makes any difference. It just amuses me."

• • •

"Because I wasn't born here, because I'm a transplant, I'm still not accepted by some of the older ones. I'm that city girl who married our local boy. I had that thrown at me last year even though I've actually lived here most of my life."

• • •

"There's a definite tension between people who have been here all their lives, or for a long time, and the new people. What often happens is that there aren't enough of the older townspeople to handle all the organizations we've got here, so they welcome any newcomers who show an interest. Now the newcomer might feel that he shouldn't volunteer for anything, but if they ask him to do a job, he accepts, then he takes off and does 18 different things. He is full of ideas and puts on a great show of interest, but the tension builds up. People feel that they are losing power, that others are taking over. There's a little resentment."

• • •

It seems to me perfectly natural and proper in a small community of enduring values and an agreed life-style that a new resident should be on probation, so to speak. Like a latecomer at a church service or the newest member of a club, he is expected to fit into the mood and rhythm of the place without causing undue disturbance. He has moved into a going concern. The town functions—as it did before he came along and as it will after he wins final acceptance in the cemetery. Its wheels turn. Before he lifts a finger on its behalf, the town services and protects him. Someone paves or plows the road by his house. Someone sweeps out the Community Hall or heats up the library. The school accepts and teaches his children. The town clerk answers his questions.

The postman delivers his mail. The firemen respond if he calls for help. All that is asked of him is that he pay his taxes and show a decent respect for the town's way of doing things. Dull conformity is not required, but he is well advised to avoid giving the impression that he wants to "improve" the town or stir up the natives. A healthy show of interest is one thing, but any display of superior knowledge or impatience with the slow, steady, Yankee-village habits of decision making will neither win friends nor influence people. There is a built-in resistance to change which is part inertia, part stubbornness and part realization that a town of this character is the creation of many lifetimes, not to be tampered with lightly.

• • •

"The way to get anything done here is to work underground. A few quiet words in the right ears can get things moving. Maybe. So much depends on the way you approach people. One thing I've noticed is this tremendous courtesy—the way people will listen to you and really seem to agree with everything you say, but then nothing happens. The powers-that-be, the town fathers, have a great capacity for delaying things—kind of putting them off until the subject just disappears. On the other hand, they can move like lightning when they want to."

• • •

"I learned when I first moved into the town that one should take care not to be too sharp. You must take a long time on the telephone. To me the biggest difference between the town and living somewhere else is that I had to completely rearrange my whole idea of what it was to be smooth and quick and so on. I was used to grabbing the phone and saying, Hey Joe, I need some information. What time is the meeting? What are they going to talk about? And so on. But you can't do it here. You've got to call up and ask how the kids are, how's the wife, what do you think of the weather? Even at a meeting, you can't get up and rattle off a lot of facts as if you were at some Ivy League or

Wall Street meeting. You can't do that here. You get up and you saunter. You can bring in the facts, but you don't use them in a way that is ostentatious in any way, that shows you know anything more than anyone else does."

•   •   •

"At first I was fascinated by the charm of the place, then I began seeing things I liked and disliked. It's only after you've been here a few years that people begin opening up and revealing some skeletons hidden in closets. There's a tremendous amount of intermarriage which has taken place among some of the older families in town. Everybody is somebody else's cousin or second cousin, aunt or uncle. The older families, those that have been around for the last hundred years, more or less, even to this day some of them are intermarrying in the same way their forefathers did. When you think about how mobile a society America is, well, it's amazing."

•   •   •

"You've got to be careful who you're talking to around here. They're all related."

•   •   •

"You'd be amazed at the way people remember things. When I first came here to live and met a lot of local people I didn't know, I would go over to my mother-in-law and ask her to clue me in a little bit on who they were. Well, the things that came out! 'Her grandmother was so and so' or 'His uncle was so and so, and he drank.' Or back in the 1920s somebody's son was queer. You hear a lot of this guilt-by-association talk. It's incredible how the history sticks on."

•   •   •

There are still great realms of empty ocean, deserts reaching to the curvature of the earth, silent, ancient forests and rocky coasts, glaciers and volcanoes, but what will we do with them? There are rich contented farms, and idyllic villages, strong barns and white-steepled churches, tree-lined streets and covered bridges, but these are residues of another time.

IAN L. MCHARG, *Design with Nature*

•   •   •

It is a strange thing to live in a residue of another time. The story of America during the past century has been the movement of masses of people from the country to the city and, more recently, from the inner city to the suburb. Nearly three quarters of all Americans now live in metropolitan areas. We are no longer a nation of farms and small towns. Yet at the beginning of the 1970s a Gallup poll of 1,505 adult Americans found that "six in ten pine for the rural life." When asked where they would prefer to live, if they could live wherever they wished, 31 percent chose a small town, 26 percent a suburb, 24 percent a farm and 18 percent a city (one percent undecided).

At the same time, a Louis Harris poll for *Life* magazine asked a cross section of 4,047 Americans to choose from among twenty-six items those things they considered most important to their happiness. "Green grass and trees around me" ranked highest of all.

"On the surface," *Life* commented, "the poll reflects an extraordinary stability, a tenacious clinging to most basic values, but combined with a willingness to adapt to the less rigid and demanding standards of the new era. . . . Americans paint an almost Jeffersonian picture of their aspirations: green grass and trees, friendly neighbors, churches, schools and good stores nearby."

•   •   •

. . . the "American Dream," the flickering images of grass, trees and "a good place for the kids to grow up." It is a dream which is presently being shattered by the cataclysmic forces of urbanization. The metropolitan countryside is beginning to emerge more and more as a nightmare. Instead of the charming little house in the country there is the monotony of uninspired development. Instead of pleasant country roads, the thoroughfares have become bizarre strips of gas station after gas station, shopping center after shopping center. Brooks have become so culverted that no one remembers them, ponds are polluted and sometimes just dry up. The landscape is festooned by high tension wires and slashed by new highways that chew up an incredible fifty acres of land per mile.

CHARLES E. LITTLE, *Challenge of the Land*

•   •   •

"I think the character of this town is going to change tremendously whether the people who live here like it or not. There's going to be a big influx of people into this area. The Greater New York Development Corporation put out a prospectus of the various areas where the city and suburbs would spread, and they've got us on the map. This is a projected thing for the next ten years. They're trying to program us."

•   •   •

"We've got to change the mentality of lots of people who have thought that bigger was better, that more was better. Now we realize that that's not so good. When I look at what's happened to the towns just south of us I kind of feel like a steamroller's coming our way. I think we ought to take some steps. Since we're bound to get some growth, I think it ought to be *orderly* growth. I don't think we're going to be hit with tremendous sudden changes, but I admit there's an element of hope in that statement. I've got my fingers crossed."

•   •   •

This whole area is of two minds about "progress." About half the people living here do so to escape progress; the other half want progress to be able to live here.

EDITORIAL

•   •   •

Progress may have been all right once, but it went on too long.

OGDEN NASH

• • •

"A Yankee Town Fears Creeping Cityhood." This is a head-line in today's *New York Times*. Guilford, in south central Connecticut, is the town in question. Its population has doubled in the past decade. Work will soon begin on the first apartments. As the farmers and fishermen fade away, businessmen and office workers move in and commute to New Haven. Parking spaces are getting scarce around the green. Vandalism is on the increase: stolen weathervanes, broken windows, overturned gravestones. Trouble with drugs and rowdy teen-agers. Some racial worries. Guilford is feeling the effects of urban sprawl, a cancerous growth, a disease called "megalopolis," which is consuming the rural quiet and country greenery all over the Atlantic coast.

• • •

Our town is well out of the way of the coastal bulldozer, but we are beginning to sense strong pressures of change coming from communities just below us. Some distance down the highway, there is a town whose increase of population from less than 1,700 to 9,000 in just two decades makes it the fastest growing in the state. And our nearest neighbor to the south is experiencing severe growing pains after more than doubling its population to 14,000 in the same span of years. It faces, according to its own newspaper, "a mind-boggling array of civic problems: more taxes, more people, more industry, and, when you get down to it, more of everything." The police force has had to be dramatically expanded to cope with crime problems more suited to a big city than a small town. Almost overnight it has been transformed from a serene country retreat, once celebrated in fiction as the place where Mr. Blandings built his dream house, to a troubled outpost of exurbia.

It is a town that has lost its innocence. More bluntly: which has allowed itself to be raped. Years and years of cranky resistance by a steadily diminishing majority of the townspeople to simple zoning regulations ("Nobody's going to tell me what I can do with my land") have left the green acres wide open to haphazard and sometimes jerry-built development. A mess has been made of some portions of the town, and a long stretch of the main highway has been turned into a third-rate Sunset Strip. The contagion of ugliness has spread, so that even on the handsome village green a stately old house will be pulled down with hardly a whimper of protest, while a huge illuminated sign is raised up on top of the biggest bank building. When some delinquent youngsters tore up parts of the village's venerable bandstand recently, it was only a sad echo of a different kind of vandalism committed and sanctioned by their elders.

• • •

Even so, our next-door neighbor is an exceptionally large township, and there is much pure landscape remaining. Thus the motorist's prelude to our town is a quarter-hour's drive through verdant countryside before crossing the line just below Bulls Bridge. There is only a small sign by the road to announce that the traveler has gone from one township into another. He must drive on for another three miles before reaching our village. He will skirt the river, pass grazing land and a few houses and barns and see the Indian reservation across the water. The low profile of the Center School comes into view across a cornfield, and then the beginning of Main Street. First a few simple clapboard houses, then the gray one-story town hall, the stately white building of the Art Association, Tobin's Garage, a small fleet of school buses and the odd assortment of structures at the crossroads. Grouped around the granite shaft of the Civil War monument, there is a splendid Victorian house, Bull's funeral home, Becker's Gulf station and St. Andrew's Episcopal Church, one of the oldest stone churches in the state. It will take the traveler less than a minute, driving at the legal limit of 30 miles per hour, to take in the rest of Main Street.

• • •

The Victorian house, still known as "old Doc Barnum's place," was almost pulled down some years ago by an oil company that meant to replace it with a gasoline station. Considerable opposition developed. It was argued that yet another filling station would make the crossroads too dangerous. "Put it up anyway," cried one citizen at town meeting, "so people can get trained for the hazards of the city in case they ever go there."

●   ●   ●

"The Civil War monument wasn't put up until 20 years after the war. My father was there as a drummer boy! He told me they had a big parade. The governor came as well as a lot of Indians. They had a cannon back of St. Andrew's shooting away, and you could hear it echoing up the river valley. One of the men from an out-of-town band was drumming so hard he broke his drumhead. The ladies of the town filled the drum full of sandwiches for them to eat on the way home."

●   ●   ●

In 1922 the state asked the town to move the monument over a few feet so that the new paved highway would not have to jog around it. At a town meeting the folks refused. They kept on refusing. The next year, as the cement advanced on the village, the highway department warned that the town was letting itself in for the cost of straightening out and paving the dirt-road jog if it ever changed its mind. It was a hotly debated issue. Much mumbling about dictatorship by state bureaucrats. But at one of the best attended town meetings ever, the people voted to move the monument. First Selectman Fred Johnson said they had made a wise decision: "Future generations will rise up and call them blessed."

●   ●   ●

Carol, age 11, has come home with an essay called "Main Street." Her English teacher has given her an A– for this "quality piece of writing which develops a strong impression and mood."

The village has only one traffic light which is at one end of Main Street. At the light is a stone monument, a tribute to the citizens of our town who fought for liberty and union. Also it is the intersection of two important roads. On one side of Main Street there is a funeral home and two groceries and the Milk Bar where you can get a Coke or sandwich. Also you would find the cleaners and the post office and the little library where you could study for a test or find a book. If you ever got sick or needed a record you could go to the drug store.

There is a railroad going through the town. By the railroad is the railroad station where you could get stationery or a present from another land for someone.

On the other side of Main Street is the Episcopal Church, covered with ivy. The whole side of the street is lined with trees in blossom and with white houses with their green lawns and spring flowers. Near the houses is the lumber yard where you can see the lumber lying out on the ground and in the background you can see the barns painted an old-fashioned red and you can hear the buzz of the chain saw cutting wood. Near the lumber yard is the hardware store and the antique store. If you walked by the restaurant you could smell the food and almost taste it in your mouth.

●   ●   ●

Just to complete the picture, we also have, south of the railroad tracks, a barbershop, the firehouse and shops for electrical goods and liquor. And over to one side, the Lawn & Garden, selling tulips and tractors. North of the tracks, there is a mixture of old and new structures: homes and barns, the Congregational church and the Community House (where we gather for fairs and auctions) and a condominium apartment project, just going up. There is also a Chevrolet dealer, insurance office, stationery, laundromat and sporting-goods shop.

Once this quarter-mile commercial stretch peters out, Main Street ends, but the highway continues north, undulating its way to Massachusetts through some of the most scenic river-valley countryside in the nation.

Backtracking to the crossroads for a moment. Should the traveler choose to head east, he would soon pass two small manufacturing plants—one making specialty transformers, the other cloth-cutting machinery—before climbing the hills to our lake region. Heading west instead, he would drive by the small savings and commercial banks, the little wooden Catholic church, the cemetery, Cliff's Garage, the new telephone building and the Mount Algo retirement home before crossing the river.

This, then, along with a few tree-lined side streets of modest homes, is the village. It is our only residential and commercial concentration, the seat of school, church and government. It is a well-furnished, workmanlike town center, pretty enough but not quite up to the postcard image of the perfect New England community wrapped around a village green. During our first century the focus of the town, village green and all, was in an area called Flanders, half a mile to the north, where prerevolutionary homes still stand. But the coming of the railroad in the 1840s completed the shift of business activities to the present village.

At that time, it was only one of several villages within the town. In the days when people had to rely on horses and their own two feet to get from place to place, we had as many as 14 school districts, and some of these were flourishing settlements with an identity all their own. A farm family struggling along at the edge of the township would seldom make the tiresome trip to Main Street.

• • •

"In some ways it appears that people had more real contact with each other in the last century. Each district of the town—Flanders, Macedonia, Bog Hollow, Skiff Mountain and the rest—had its own personality, its own school and small stores, which depended on the center a great deal. You can tell in the old letters that there was constant information about what was going on in the different areas. Although there was time-consuming driving distance, they were in close contact with each other. Apparently politics affected them all. They were all part of the various parties that existed then, and the political antagonisms were hot and heavy."

• • •

"I've been living in the town all my life—born right on Main Street, which makes me a city girl, I suppose, compared to the hill families. I've seen all sorts of little changes. Some old houses have come down. There was a drugstore where the bank is now. The post office was in Watson's, which used to be a general store. The present post office was a hall for dancing and meetings. John Judd's farm was right on Main Street, where the lumberyard is now. Tobacco used to be grown right in the center of town, but that's all gone now."

• • •

"It is true that our population in the 1930s, during the Depression, was half of what it is now, but, well, you weren't aware of it. It was busy in the town. We had more buildings on Main Street than you have now, and of course more trees. We used to have a lot of inns, but they disappeared one by one. Just south of Crawford's store, there was a big house, an inn, where there is a vacant lot now. There was an inn where the library is and an inn on the corner by the monument, replaced by the Gulf station. They cut down several fine old black walnut trees there. Only one is still standing, all paved around. Big houses on Main Street like the Kassam house and the Judd house have been torn down. Too big, I guess, for modern times. Taxes too high to make it worthwhile keeping them. It's a shame to see them go, though."

• • •

"There used to be a lot of activity in town. The trains passing through every day. People staying in the little hotels. The horse teams would go up and down hauling stuff. Everybody had chickens. Most had a pig. There was farming right in the center of town. Most people had a horse and an icehouse. One of the store owners, Henry Mosher, said when he was a boy everybody butchered and everybody had hens. When he started a store, he used to sell a big barrel of salt pork every year. Then just a half-barrel. Finally nothing. He used to sell codfish too. Henry was quite a fellow. He was the town clerk and everything else. He had a nice chair out in front of the store, and if anybody came to the store he'd ask them what they wanted before he got up. He hoped he didn't have it."

• • •

"When I was a youngster in town they sold everything you could imagine in Watson's. It sells hardware and clothing now, but it used to be a real old-fashioned general store. Food, tools, medicine, stamps, boots, candles—everything. They used to open about five thirty in the morning and stay open until eleven at night. After eight o'clock at night they never sold anything, but it was the gathering place for the town. I remember when they had a potbellied stove in there with a sandbox around it. More Presidents of the United States have been elected in Watson's than in any place in the country. I mean that."

• • •

"Nelson Watson was the son of a Connecticut peddler, a man who went around selling things off a horse and wagon. I used to say that you could go into Watson's with nothing but a barrel around you and come out fully dressed carrying meat and groceries, tires for your car, and anything else you needed."

• • •

I get the impression that there is less commotion in the middle of town these days even though our population has been rising steadily since the Depression and the number of cars has doubled in the last 20 years. The virtual closing down of the railroad has made a difference. Housewives with freezers at home go to market less often, and the automobile gives them a chance to shop in the larger towns, where prices are lower in the supermarkets.

"You're lucky up on the mountain," someone told me, a little peevishly. "Here on Main Street we have traffic, noise and dust. Don't forget that we don't all live in pure country surroundings." Maybe so, but anyone up from the city could only be impressed by the country flavor of our little downtown. In the fall, pumpkins are placed on the verandahs, and Indian corn is hooked on front doors. Right now, flowers and baby trees are set out for sale in front of the Lawn & Garden and the grocery stores. One of the local girls can be seen exercising her horse in the field across from the Congregational church. With the approach of summer, we will be selling books on tables in front of the library and holding fairs and bake sales at the Community House—spilling out on the lawn if the weather is agreeable. Every so often hikers with backpacks come trudging through the village. If they are heading north we suggest that they take their rest at the waterfall about four miles up the road.

• • •

A big meeting tonight in the school gymnasium. This is a hearing called by the Planning and Zoning Commission to sound out the public once again on the most controversial issue to hit the town in many a year. It has to do with a 106-acre ski area that a group of outside developers would like to build on a mountainside about half a mile south of the waterfall.

Feelings run deep. Much bitterness in the air. Angriest are the people living nearest to the proposed ski slopes. They would be particularly affected by the increase of traffic and other invasions of their tranquil surroundings. At dinner parties I have been accused of circulating a pro-ski-area petition. As a matter of fact, I am still making up my mind. "How would *you* like it if someone built a ski resort in *your* backyard?" asked the man who pinned me against a wall one night. The people who favor the development, of course, speak of recreational values, the preservation of open space, new business, jobs and fresh tax money flowing into the town treasury.

"The trick is to get land uses," says the local editor, "which, while paying taxes, make little or no demand on the town for services." But at an emotion-charged public hearing last year, soon after the ski idea was announced, there was much talk about the noise of snow-making machinery, "people pollution" and the danger of "ski bums and LSD people peeking in our windows." Inevitably, because the very notion of local planning and zoning raises the specter of socialism in some minds, someone spoke out in favor of free enterprise: "These men plan to put up their own money. They could make a profit or they could get a loss. But they try. That's the American way. That's why we were able to put men on the moon."

When the town adopted zoning some years ago, just in time to head off the creation of a junkyard on a scenic stretch of road, an elaborate set of regulations was drawn up to cover every kind of land use from riding stables and nursing homes to bowling alleys and golf courses. Unaccountably, nothing was said about a ski area, and the Planning and Zoning Commission has spent some months now on an amendment that would permit ski developments but only under stringent conditions. At the last stormy meeting, in fact, the commission's first attempt at an amendment was denounced as being so tough that "it prevents what it purports to allow." The commissioners went back to their drawing boards.

At tonight's session we have had an hour and a half of spirited debate about the latest proposed amendment. Some heckling, some angry outbursts, but the anti-ski forces seem to know that the majority of the townspeople favor a strictly regulated development. "And suppose," said one lady, making a last-ditch stand, "all the snow-making activity lowers the water table and my well runs dry?"

The commissioners thank us for our views and go into closed session. Then they emerge to announce that they have voted unanimously for adoption of the amendment. No doubt the nearby property-owners will seek ways to block it in the courts, but it looks as though skiing will be added one day to our What-is-it? economy.

*   *   *

The ski-area dispute says a lot about our decision-making process. There is much more to it than the infrequent town meetings. Any matter that involves major spending or a significant change in our customary way of doing things is thrashed out for weeks and months and occasionally even years before it is settled. We either talk it to death or prove it worthy of adoption. As in the case of the ski project, or the sewer and school-expansion issues, we argue at meetings and hearings, pass around petitions, buttonhole the selectmen, write letters to the newspaper and keep on sounding out our fellow townsmen. Along the way some original misconceptions and exaggerated fears and hopes are weeded out. Fresh information is revealed. Some people change their minds, others dig in their heels. Eventually something emerges that most of us can live with, and by that time we are too tired to care.

*   *   *

The town clerk reports that she has sold a total of 116 fishing licenses during April. It is that time of the year. The state gets most of the money, over $500, but the town keeps $40.60 for its trouble.

*   *   *

Sign in the post office:
CANADA LILY.
THIS PLANT IS ON THE
CONNECTICUT PRESERVATION LIST.
IT IS RAPIDLY BECOMING RARE.
LOVE IT. LEAVE IT.

*   *   *

A Sunday morning in April. Bright sun, light breeze, sweet smell of spring. We drive down to the parsonage for a tree-planting ceremony. Jan, the eldest of our four children, is in charge. She and classmates at the high school are greatly involved

in the ecology movement; their organization is called New E.R.A.
—Environmental Rescue Alliance. This community has far more
trees than most places, and by all appearances we take pains not
to misuse the gifts of nature, but this planting exercise is simply
a way of saying that we care greatly about the natural world. The
slim young maple and the little ash were dug out of our own
woods and carried gently down the mountain. It is satisfying to
think that they will provide beauty and shade, long after we are
gone, in this quiet country churchyard.

    •   •   •

For you shall go out with joy, and be led forth with peace: the
mountains and the hills shall break forth before you into singing, and
all the trees of the field shall clap their hands.

ISAIAH 55:12

    •   •   •

According to David Van Vleck, a Middlebury College biology
professor who has been visiting us over the weekend, the country
is rapidly being paved over. There were 13 acres of arable and
forest land for every person in the United States in 1900. Now
there are six acres. The projection for the year 2000 is two
acres. America's highways already cover an area equal to the
size of Delaware, Rhode Island, Vermont, Massachusetts and
Connecticut.

    •   •   •

"Think'st thou, Pierre, the time will ever come when all the earth shall
be paved?"

"Thank God, that can never be!"

HERMAN MELVILLE, Pierre

    •   •   •

A miasmic cloud rises from every Connecticut city and blackens the
clear blue sky above. This is the awesome reflection of the population
explosion of men and machines wracking the city below. A city-bound

traveler cresting the hill nearby is suddenly confronted with the cloud
hanging over the city. He shudders as his car rolls down the hill and
into that man-made muck. As his lungs begin to suck it in, he worries.
He cogitates. In creating the automobile he rides in and building the
stacks that make megalopolis possible, has he rubbed Aladdin's lamp?
Is that giant cloud a jinni that he can no longer control? Will the
lights flicker out, smothered in smog? Will the population explosion
rip apart his arduously assembled societal machinery and cause it one
day to run wild and out of control? . . .

Even the tobacco plants have been signalling us here in Connecticut
since 1950. That year they told us that smog had arrived in Connecticut. At first the plant scientists missed the signal, too. Not knowing
then that ozone from cars is the cause, the scientists called the disease
"weather fleck."

Benefiting from the wonderful wisdom of hindsight, however, they
now know that it should have been called just "fleck" because the
weather as provided by God had simply not changed that much. It is
now clear that man, not God, had changed the weather. Through the
flatulence of their cars and the belching of their stacks the citizens of
Hartford and other cities were pouring tons of stuff into the air and
changing the weather in the nearby Tobacco Valley. The plants complained, but few men really heard the signal until nearly 20 years had
passed.

REPORT OF THE GOVERNOR'S COMMITTEE
ON ENVIRONMENTAL POLICY, 1970

•   •   •

The Audubon Center is a quarter-hour drive from our house,
going by way of the back roads and keeping a sharp eye out for
raccoons. On my last visit, I looked over an ecology exhibition and
jotted down a question that had been posed to a group of children: "The human population is rapidly rising and so is our use
of natural resources and the production of pollution. We may
even go extinct! So what?"
The answers of three children:

—So what! The world is being polluted! And it's going to be cleaned
up. And if it isn't, we're all going to die.

—Everything takes its own course. If this is meant to happen it will. There may be another world born because in time this one is going to be demolished.

—So what if it happens? It happens there is no solution. We can't do anything that would really help. If we became extinct all the other problems would be solved.

• • •

Children are growing up in New York who have never seen the Milky Way.

The New Yorker

• • •

"Do you know what's really *amazing* about this town? You can come in and look around and think that there's nothing to do here. No movie house, no bowling alley, not even a drive-in if you want to get a hamburger. You've got to drive half an hour for anything like that. Go through town at night and the place is dead. Somebody polishing the fire engine is about all the life you'll see. But have you ever counted up how many organizations we've got here, and all the times they meet? If you're a socially interested person you've got an incredible choice. And if you're not, we leave you alone."

• • •

"What I think is best about a town like this, we're in a community where one is not just a digit or a number but one is a person, who is recognized by most people. At least recognized by the merchants, and the post office, and so on. There is a certain human element, so that you can go downtown and feel like you're accepted. When you move into the town, there is knowledge of the move. It filters through the community. And if you want to you can make an impact fairly quickly. If you, for instance, go to the zoning and other meetings, showing an interest, this gets around. People say, Did you see who was at that meeting? and, Who was that person? Or at any church gathering or anything else like that, you can pretty much pick out who's new and then go over and say hello. You get immediate response. You can fit right in, right away. There's one new family in town who complained to me, panning the community because they said nobody had stopped in. I said, 'Look, it's up to you. You've really got to get out, go to these meetings. If you see a church supper, go! If you see this fair or this PTA meeting or anything else, go to it!' "

•   •   •

"I think you have to distinguish between the people who come out here to have a nice country home and maybe get away from their city jobs and who don't really want to be involved in local affairs, and those who come out here with some skill or interest that they could bring to the town and they want to use it. This town has so many organizations and so many affairs going on that you couldn't possibly just rely on the people who have spent most of their lives here. We've got to work with the newcomers. It's the same problem for both political parties. After all, very few of the offices are sought. For both town political committees it's a matter of getting people who are willing to take the jobs."

•   •   •

It is the extended network of voluntary associations which has been the source of so much independent initiative, in politics and social life, in the United States. One might argue that with our increasing urbanization such civic consciousness would diminish. And yet I would argue to the contrary. In American life today there is probably more voluntary association, more local community and suburban newspapers and more participation in organizations, professional, hobby and civic, than at any previous period.

DANIEL BELL

•   •   •

The socially or politically interested person can run himself ragged just going to meetings, serving on committees and doing all the volunteer work that helps keep the town alive and kicking. It is a wonder that there are enough adults available to fill all the offices of all the town boards and commissions, all the church groups and all the service and social organizations. Some people, of course, seem to do everything. They make up for those who do nothing. There are certain individuals, and even whole families, who can always be relied on to take minutes, bring flowers, recruit members, collect money, speak up at the PTA, boil hot dogs at a Community House fair, bake a casserole for the church supper, drive young people to a youth conference and call on the old lady who has not been seen in the village lately.

The busier they are, the more they seem able to take on and the more they are asked to do. For all the complaining that people do about the way the welfare state is wiping out individual initiative and effort, there appears to be more demand than ever for volunteer services. And not just locally. Many of the same people who are so much involved in community affairs are meeting about planned parenthood, working to save the environment, organizing for consumer protection and otherwise taking part in national health and education campaigns. Few weeks go by when somebody isn't raising money for something.

• • •

A list of the town associations should include the chamber of commerce, fire department, Parent-Teachers Association, Republican and Democratic town committees, Memorial Library, Art Association, Grange, Order of the Eastern Star, Homemakers, Nursing Association, Chess Club, Garden Club, FISH (emergency social service), KEEP (environmental education), Historical Society, Informal Club, American Legion, Alcoholics Anonymous, Boy Scouts, Girl Scouts and St. Luke's Lodge of the Masons. But that's not all.

• • •

Since its first meeting St. Luke's has met on the Thursday on or before the Full Moon and still does. Most all of the old Lodges called their meetings on or near the Full Moon so that they could see to get around easily as many times they had several miles to drive and in those days they drove a horse over poor roads and not an automobile with bright lights on a nice smooth road.

CLIFFORD C. SPOONER, 1939

• • •

"You know what puzzles me? How a town this size can raise the amount of money it raises every year for all these causes and drives. We seldom go under our quota for whatever it is—Nursing Association, Episcopal fair, Red Cross, library, and so on. But there's just too many things you have to give to."

• • •

"One of the best forces for good in this town when I moved in, many years ago, was a group of intellectual old maids. There was a long period of time when the New England old maid was written about a great deal. They were all college-bred girls who were so superior to the men they could have married that they stayed single. Well, we had half a dozen or so of them, related, who had a very fine influence. They got the library built and organized, and many other things. They were strong in the zoning fight. Even before zoning came in they put over the ordinances which have saved us from billboards and flashy signs. They were a real blessing to the town, these highly educated women."

• • •

The town owes much to its leading citizens, guiding spirits, prime movers and opinionated activists—the spark plugs of its engine. But it needs as well its quiet, plodding, workaday, seldom-noticed citizens. When death comes, they make a brief posthumous impact, a final claim for recognition, and the preachers struggle for words to describe the meaning of their unremarkable lives. These thoughts come to me after chancing upon the obituary of Miles Bordwell, who died here in 1864 as the little-known son of the well-known Reverend Joel Bordwell.

He was born on the first of September, 1775, in the house in which he died, and his long life of 89 years was spent upon the farm which had been the possession of his father. He was never married, but lived, after the death of his parents, with a maiden sister. For almost 40 years that household remained unchanged. A brother, sister, and a faithful domestic, dwelt together in the quiet simplicity which marked the former days of New England. He never sought office, nor took part in public life, but devoted himself to the cultivation of his farm. Ever most upright and a constant attendant upon public worship, it was not till he had reached the age of 63 that he made a public profession of his faith in Christ. His natural diffidence kept him from active service in the church but he adorned his profession by an unblamable life and by many deeds of Christian charity.

• • •

These are strange spring days. The temperature has shot way up, and we have been outdoors in our shirt sleeves, throwing a baseball around, but there are still piles of snow behind the barn and down by the creek. I see people fixing up their canoes and sailboats, but we are still getting some below-freezing nights. It is too early to take off the snow tires.

• • •

For a century after it was founded in 1801, the local Association for Detecting Horse Thieves was one of the town's most formidable organizations. Formed "for the purpose of the pursuit, detection and apprehension of horse thieves and the recovery of stolen horses," the association was still going strong in 1895 with dues of five dollars a year, businesslike bylaws, a healthy bank account and sixty members. Pursuers were bidden "at all times to hold themselves in readiness" to set out immediately when warned by a member of the executive committee.

• • •

"You can see that we still have a firehouse crowd. They gather there, same as always, but I don't suppose it is quite the social club we used to have in the old days. Way back, the first fire department had about 30 people in it, and 29 of them were 60 years old or better. They had a little old reel and about 200 feet of hose. And when the fire alarm rang—well, they used a steel tire that had come off a locomotive. It was hung between two poles and a crosspiece and they'd sledgehammer it on the side. Everybody came down to the firehouse and grabbed the tool he liked best and went off to the fire with it. Of course, everything would burn up. You couldn't do much with 200 feet of hose and a little old reel."

* * *

I have often admired the extreme skill with which the inhabitants of the United States succeed in proposing a common object for the exertions of a great many men and inducing them voluntarily to pursue it.

ALEXIS DE TOCQUEVILLE

* * *

During the greater part of the life of the town there was no organized means of fire fighting. There was little hope of saving a burning home or barn once a blaze was well started. The fire department had its origins in the formation of a water company in 1881 to supply the village—the central commercial district— with water. This led to the creation of a fire association, char- tered by the Connecticut General Assembly, to provide for the protection of the village (now known as the "fire district") and for basic services. The present fire department began in 1911 as a hose company. A converted barn was used as a firehouse until the volunteers built the present two-story brick building 40 years later.

* * *

It is something of an honor to be asked to join the fire depart- ment. The firehouse serves, of course, as a social club, good for card games and the kind of talk that used to be heard around the cracker barrel, but the firemen take their work seriously. Those of us who have had our homes saved by the volunteers know how capable they are. They keep their equipment in top condition, arrange regular drills, hold postmortems after important fires and test their skill in competitions with other volunteer forces at firemen's fairs. The town provides some support to the firemen each year, but they raise most of their funds themselves —ten thousand dollars or so—at an annual spring ball and summer carnival.

*　*　*

Last year the volunteers answered forty-two calls. There were six building fires, nine brush fires, two electrical fires, six automobile fires, 18 "still" alarms (situations handled without calling out the full force) and one false alarm.

*　*　*

There are some 200,000 paid firemen in the United States and one and a half million volunteer firemen. There are less than 2,000 full-time paid fire departments and more than 20,000 volunteer fire departments. Despite the increasingly urban character of American life and the erosion of individual and community self-reliance, fully half of the American people live in rural and suburban places that rely on volunteer firemen for protection. Economy is the chief reason. Even for a large and prosperous suburb, the salary cost alone of a three-shift professional fire department is a few hundred thousand dollars too much to bear. And then, there is something about a volunteer service which goes to the core of a community's sense of community. We have traveled far beyond the days of communal barn raisings and husking bees, but we still have, in much of America, volunteer firemen to remind us of our ability to serve one another.

*　*　*

"Gosh, the railroad is certainly petering out. You can see it getting old. The ties—you can walk along them and push your cane down into the puffy old ties and everything. They bring down these heavy transformers. Fellow told me the other day when they come down they can't exceed 20 miles an hour. They're afraid the bridge won't take it. And if they go less than 20 miles an hour they're afraid the track will give way and the thing will get to rocking."

•   •   •

Our railroad is on its last legs, or rails. Ever since the 1840s the inhabitants of these towns have been able to go north by train to Massachusetts and south to Connecticut cities and on to New York. Earlier in this century the journey to Grand Central Station was considerably faster than it is today. Normally, however, the townspeople would just travel a few stations up and down the line to shop, go to school, visit the dentist, call on friends, take in the movies. Then the automobile and the truck came along in ever greater numbers, and railroad service, both passenger and freight, deteriorated. Fewer people came to town by train. The Main Street inns closed up. The railroad station shut its doors. Although a daily freight still comes through town, passenger service is down to two weekend trains in each direction: forlorn single carriages looking like lost Toonerville trolleys. Now the Penn Central has posted a notice on the outside of the stations all along the route announcing its plans to discontinue all passenger service in a matter of weeks. We still have a little time to protest, but it looks like a lost cause.

•   •   •

End of innocence note. The children in the town have been used to leaving their bicycles, sleds, wagons and such things outdoors, often overnight, sometimes by the roadside, without worrying about it. But there has been some stealing lately, and a juvenile in another town has been arrested for taking a bike from here. The resident state trooper has put out a notice asking the youngsters not to leave their bicycles unattended, especially by the main roads.

•   •   •

Now the days stretch out at both ends. The May sun stays with us right through supper, and we have begun to eat outdoors again, on the warmest days, sitting at the battered old trestle table that was all but buried in snow a brief while ago. Now the horses stay out in the pastures through the night, and we are done with shoveling manure from the stalls. Eric has moved the last of the skis and snow shovels from the mudroom to the barn. The corn popper has been replaced in the kitchen by the flyswatter. The snow blower has given way to the mower on the small tractor. We put up the screens in place of the storm windows and churn up the vegetable garden with a rented Roto-Tiller. We have to hustle to keep up with the grass, which is springing out of the ground faster than we can cut it. It is a burgeoning, blossoming, bird-filled spring world, both beautiful and demanding.

•   •   •

The city man in the country on a May morning is like a child on Christmas Day: bewildered by the distracting abundance, he doesn't know where to begin; the sudden richness of life is frustrating; he almost wants to cry.

LEWIS GANNETT, *Cream Hill*

•   •   •

Tonight we held what must have been the shortest annual budget meeting in the town's history. Forty-four citizens, a good many of them officials, gathered in the Center School gymnasium and within seven minutes unanimously approved a budget of $770,080.35, an increase of nearly $100,000 over the previous year. There was no discussion. All cut-and-dried. We had done our complaining and explaining at the budget hearing two weeks ago. At that time, various concerned taxpayers wanted to know why there was so much spending. The First Selectman and other officials explained that they had clamped down on expenditures as much as possible but costs were rising everywhere and the town had acquired an annual debt burden of more than $50,000 in interest on the big loans for the sewer and the school addition.

The budget shows that education accounts for nearly two thirds of the town's expenses. The figure is $458,300. Just transporting the children to school costs us $44,000 a year. The work of keeping the roads in shape accounts for the second largest spending item. It is clear that the town budget will reach a million dollars in a very few years.

• • •

My village used to raise corn and hay but the only thing it raises now is taxes.

ERIC SLOANE

• • •

"I've been thinking about writing a letter to the paper. I just get so upset about people who think the most important thing is to fight against any increase in taxes. It doesn't matter what it is —if it means more taxes, they're against it. But I *want* children in this town to get a good education, and I *want* good services and a clean environment. You don't get it for free. If it means more taxes, then I'm willing to pay. If it means I have to reduce my own standard of living to keep this town a decent place to live, then I'll do that too. Taxes don't frighten me!"

• • •

Well, taxes frighten some people. We know that we are better off than most city dwellers and suburbanites, judging by what we read in the papers, but we have seen local taxes (quite apart from all the other taxes we pay) double within the past decade. Right after tonight's budget meeting the Board of Finance met and set a new mill rate of 44, meaning we'll be taxed $44 for each $1,000 of the assessed value of property. This is a sharp increase over the prevailing rate of 39.5. Our new tax bills, starting in July, will be up by 12 percent or so.

Local property taxes bring in two thirds of the town's annual income. State grants for schools, roads and a few other things account for most of the rest. Property means land, buildings, automobiles, cattle and other basic items as well as business inventories, machinery and equipment. Each taxpayer goes down to the town hall once a year to account for his property, and from all of this the board of assessors produces its Grand List of the assessed value (not the market value) of all the taxable property in the town. The current net valuation is $12,282,833. The gross valuation is a quarter-million dollars more, but war veterans and the elderly are given certain reductions. The assessors, of course, decide the property values, and there is a Board of Tax Review standing by to hear complaints.

• • •

It all seems fair enough, and we know that there's no avoiding the tax burden, but it still hurts. One common grievance is that 40 percent of the property in the town is exempt from taxation. This includes the several thousand acres of state parks and forests, the resources of the churches and benevolent organizations and the considerable holdings of the two boarding schools. There is quite a bit of grumbling directed at the schools even though they do pay taxes on their residential property—and incidentally provide jobs and help local business.

We are on the lookout, of course, for the kind of additional industry which would somehow be virtuous enough to take on some of the tax load without polluting the atmosphere or otherwise upsetting the rustic mood. The chamber of commerce during the 16 years of its existence has had some success in these matters, bringing in the first new industrial activities since the iron companies died out at the end of the last century. It is now hunting for another manufacturing plant or some sort of commercial development. The townspeople look on with mixed emotions. They know by the experience of other places that a big new project can create fresh financial problems while easing others. What is most feared is anything that might ultimately place heavy demands on the town's services, particularly the school system. They had trouble enough getting the new school addition approved and financed.

•   •   •

I notice, on this sunny May morning of bird songs and spring breezes, that the lawn is sprinkled with violets and dandelions. The driveway is carpeted, as if in the wake of a brief snowstorm, with crab apple blossoms.

•   •   •

THE WORLD CRUMBLES?
SERVICE TO BE HELD HERE
THIS SATURDAY NOON

HEADLINE

•   •   •

"We haven't lived here too long, but we love it. You have open spaces for the kids to grow up. The only thing is: I feel I should only stay if I keep on being aware of the things that are going on and being actively involved. If I thought I was with-drawing, being very happy here and ignoring responsibilities un-der my nose, then I would say it's time to move on."

•   •   •

The critical events of the past several days leave us all in a state of un-certain turmoil. A service of prayer and meditation for our world situation will be held at the First Congregational Church at 12:00 noon on Saturday. All who are deeply pained by the world crises are invited to expose themselves to God's word of judgment and mercy in the hope that the new vision and direction may guide our feeling and action.

ANNOUNCEMENT

•   •   •

"We get more bad news now than we used to. It's hard to say whether people are any happier today, or less happy, than they used to be. All I know is, we get more bad news. You get New York and the whole world on television. We used to worry about our neighbors and the village. Now we have to worry about the whole planet. Once in a while we get some sad news here in town, but every night we have to listen to the troubles of the world."

●　●　●

There is not much bad news in *The Good Times Dispatch.* "Devoted to the militant practice of independent journalism," the paper calls itself "a little local weekly with readers around the world." It sells for ten cents. Readers get 16 or so magazine-sized offset-printed pages of news and views (sometimes it is hard to tell which is which) and advertisements for everything from cube steaks to chain saws. A classified ad costs 75 cents for an across-the-page line. "The publishers trust users to figure— and remit what they owe. THE HONOR SYSTEM prevails."

The paper was born 20 years ago as the mimeographed journal of Boy Scout Troop 11. It had 22 amateur reporters and was known as *The Good Turn Daily.* It was said to be the only weekly daily in the country. Volume 1, Number 1, is sealed with other articles in the cornerstone of the local telephone building. On one memorable occasion a line in a senior citizen's poem about "sunning in the hay" was transformed into "sinning in the hay."

When the amateur paper got too big for its britches, its professional advisers, who had come to town after considerable experience in journalism, turned it into a successful commercial enterprise. They are outspoken and opinionated, as editors ought to be. They have stepped on toes all over town, and some people swear they never read the paper, though they probably do on the sly. The more generous-minded note that the editors keep their letters columns wide open to all, even to those who lambaste them, and that they serve every organization in town as a free bulletin board for announcements of meetings, socials, fairs and fund-raising drives.

• • •

I have often thought that nothing would do more extensive good at small expense than the establishment of a small circulating library in every county, to consist of a few well-chosen books, to be lent to the people of the county, under such regulations as would secure their safe return in due time.

THOMAS JEFFERSON

• • •

"You ought to know a little history of the town library. There used to be an inn on that spot where people riding the railroad used to stop. When it burned down they just left the cellar hole. It was used for a dump. You just dumped your garbage in the hole. Later on we covered it up and built the library. The architect designed it after he took a trip to Virginia. It's like a little brick house you could find in Williamsburg."

• • •

Our Memorial Library has grown a bit since it was started in a local home in 1915, and since the little brick building was built seven years later. During the postwar period the number of volumes has risen from 4,000 to 15,000, and the annual circulation of books (at both the main library and the Center School branch) is now 45,000. All of which suggests that a good many people here still read books, despite talking furniture, as Fred Allen once described television to me. The library is bursting at the seams. Our librarian has somehow contrived to find room for the rising tide of books and periodicals and to squeeze in the pint-sized readers in the children's attic, as well as the teen-agers doing their homework, the housewives desperate for the latest best seller, the senior citizens meeting for coffee, and the regular bookworms. It is obvious, however, that a fund-raising drive will have to be launched soon to produce more space.

• • •

Although it is a free public library, it is operated not by the town government but by a local library association, which recruits dues-paying members. Major support comes from the annual town grant of $6,000, as well as from membership dues and a small state grant, but the additional thousand dollars or so produced by the library fair keeps the institution afloat. This is one of our major events of the year, not so exciting or prolonged as the firemen's fair and not so lucrative as the Sacred Heart fair (which makes good use of raffles and wheels of fortune), but cozy, friendly and good fun. It is a worthy successor to the street fairs of the 1920s which raised the money to build the library in the first place.

Today, as it happens, has been library-fair day, and a good many of us are now in an advanced state of Saturday afternoon postfair exhaustion. Although the thing takes many weeks to organize, it physically begins to take shape when the men of the road crew bring a truckload of long wooden tables to the Community House. Volunteer workers prepare for the selling of baked goods, plants and flowers, old and new books, refreshments and those household rejects known as white elephants. This morning, as usual, the doors flew open at ten o'clock and the waiting crowd poured in. For nearly four hours the townspeople and visitors surged in and out, munching hot dogs, searching for rare books, parking their children in the basement kiddieland, and looking over the geraniums, cherry pies and bargain junk. On the stage: a pictorial exhibit of the town's history. On the front lawn: children's games, an antique fire engine, a clothesline art show, a local artist doing portrait sketches, and an event billed as the High Noon Egg-Dropping Spectacular.

At the stroke of twelve the fair chairman climbed to the top rungs of a ladder and began hurling fresh, uncooked and presumably fragile eggs a great distance as the assembled children and bemused adults cheered and moaned. Only five out of 18 eggs broke as they struck the grassy ground. The rest just bounced, thus demonstrating anew the wondrous structural properties of the egg. This somewhat zany exhibition was a

money-raising exercise, something special at this year's fair, but
city people driving through town and seeing the country folk
at play might well have decided that this was some strange native
custom.

* * *

A small country town is not the place in which one would choose to
quarrel with a wife; every human being in such places is a spy.

SAMUEL JOHNSON

* * *

"Privacy? Well, there's no privacy in the sense that everyone
here gets to know everything about you—or just about everything. Which in some respects is good, and some bad. The privacy comes from your not letting out what you don't want to
be known."

* * *

Dear Editor:

Would you kindly print the enclosed letter so that my neighbors will
not continue to be annoyed by gossips wanting information.

For those of you who get your thrills for the day with your ugly
malicious tongues, let me give you the story first hand. . . .

The Good Times Dispatch

* * *

"There's a grapevine in this town. It's a real winding snake.
It turns all over the town and is transferred by one, and by a
phone call to another, and it goes around like wildfire."

* * *

"It's a great town for rumors. I was said to be pregnant when
we were married, but it took me three and a half years to
oblige."

* * *

"A lot of gossip comes via some old gals whose husbands have died and they're sitting in the house. One in particular, who's dead now, had been in a wheelchair for years and never went out, but she had that phone going—and I'm telling you! I heard about the time she fell out of the wheelchair and some people who took care of her sometimes, because she lived alone, came along, and while they were picking her up she had 40 different stories to tell. It wasn't stuff out of the newspaper, because it hadn't reached the newspaper yet. It was all off the telephone, and to think there were people saying, 'Oh, this poor old lady who lives alone and never sees anybody.' This was her biggest disaster in falling out of the wheelchair—that she couldn't get on the phone."

●   ●   ●

Memorial Day. The town shows the flag and pays its respects to the "fallen heroes" of many wars. It is a sunshine-perfect day for drums and bugles, the Stars and Stripes and solemn moments of prayer. The parade starts off at the Center School after lunch: the school band, veterans, ministers, Boy Scouts, Girl Scouts and the volunteer firemen in their red jackets and white slacks. Children scamper along the sidewalks and hitch a ride on the old fire truck. There are moving ceremonies at the two church grave-yards and salutes of rifle fire. Just for an instant we sniff the smoke of battle. A Boy Scout reads the Gettysburg Address to an assembly on Main Street. The marchers finally troop back to the schoolyard and furl their flags while the excited youngsters line up for ice cream.

●   ●   ●

A Sunday walk in the woods with the girls. Dazzling sun, cool shade, the spring air effervescent. We cross the hayfield, pass through the pine grove and step gingerly from rock to rock across the stream just above the little waterfall. We stop to ad-mire the architecture of the beavers before going on through the birches to the horse trail. Julie identifies the trees and flowers and ferns for me. Carol, who cares about the world, is shocked to find a beer can. She picks it up to carry it all the way home for proper disposal. We pause to gather clumps of moss. We hear the wail of a train, an almost alien sound from far down in the river valley. From a high point on the trail, where great gray slabs of rock rise from the ground, we can see distant green pastures and the golden weathervane swinging above our red barn. Looking down at our feet, we read the words painted on the stone by two unknown walkers in the woods of another year.

LYALL AND ADKINS
DEDICATE
THIS ROCK TO
NATURE, LIBERTY AND HAPPINESS

• • •

Commencement exercises at the Center School. Thirty boys and girls ready to be graduated. A scrubbed, combed and shining new generation, they sit in neat rows at the front of the gymnasium, facing their beaming parents and teachers across a bank of flowers. It is a touching ceremony, perhaps because it is so familiar and predictable, from the "Pomp and Circumstance" processional to "Auld Lang Syne" and the benediction. There is a strong emphasis on patriotism and traditional values: the call to the colors, the pledge of allegiance, the national anthem, awards presented by the American Legion and the Veterans of Foreign Wars, and a Freedom Award from the local newspaper. Yet there is more than a hint that these pupils are not just little carbon copies of their parents. The style of hair and the songs from *Hair*, so rousingly sung by the glee club, are something special. And the themes of the speakers and winning essayists reveal an awareness and knowledgeability of the world's ills which belie their years. "Responsible Protest for a Better America" is the theme of one graduate's paper. "Never for the sake of peace and quiet,"

says another, quoting Dag Hammarskjöld, "deny your own con-
victions."

• • •

Three days later we attend the outdoor commencement at the
six-town high school. It is a muggy day with threatening skies.
Of the 168 graduates, only 26 are from our small town, but they
contribute the salutatorian and three of the four other student
speakers, and they win more than their share of the awards and
honors. Here, too, the proceedings are traditional and patriotic,
but a certain rebelliousness is evident. Several students wear the
peace symbol on their black gowns and balk at reciting the Oath
of Athenian Youth ("We will revere and obey the community's
laws . . .") or singing "The Star-Spangled Banner" (". . . the
bombs bursting in air . . ."). The shoulder-length hair of a few
young men no doubt discomforts some of the assembled adults.
But the ceremony could hardly be more decorous as we listen to
the orators sing "America the Beautiful" and applaud the graduates filing by to receive their diplomas. It all ends on a high
note of joyful liberation and fond farewell.

• • •

Late June. Promises fulfilled. These are magnificent balmy
days. We open the doors and windows and let the perfect
weather indoors. But it is hard to get any work done when the
breezes bring such heady fragrances and such enticing late-spring
sounds. At night, rocking in the dark on the verandah, we can
hear the drumming of insects against the screens of lighted rooms.
The children stay up later nowadays and sleep later in the morning, no longer worrying about the usual mad rush to make the
school bus in time. They laze about the house, weed for a while
in the garden and make plans for a picnic. June has brought us
fireflies and butterflies (though far fewer than there used to be,
the old-timers say) and such an outburst of green growth that the
horse-trails have turned into jungle paths. Around town the students have come home from college, the softball team is on a

winning streak, vacation church-school has begun and swimming classes are going on down at Emery Park. The hills are filling up with summer people, but the pace of life is slowing down. We are ready for the ripeness of summer.

SUMMER

THE CHILDREN keep bringing home wounded robins. They give me a medical report: "George I is thriving. George II eaten by a rat. George III thriving. George IV simply died."

• • •

Birds play a large role in our country life. They are our closest and busiest neighbors. From time to time, when the season is right, we walk around the local ponds to watch the ducks and Canadian geese. Sometimes we join the Audubon crowd on a hawk watch. The dog is forever quarreling with the birds in the trees, and the patient cat lies in constant wait for a careless blue jay. The peevish barn swallows swoop down on us whenever we come near their nests in the nooks of the horse stalls. And there is a frenzy of escaping birds every time we step into the hayloft. We hear woodpeckers at work, and every so often we meet an owl. Sometimes we see pheasants skittering through the woods. We keep a pair of binoculars handy to watch the succession of fine-feathered friends at the backyard feeder, and a scorecard is kept. I have just brought it upstairs from the kitchen drawer.

Robin
Cardinal
Blue Jay
Goldfinch
Downy Woodpecker

Purple Finch
House Sparrow
Field Sparrow
Wood Thrush
Black-capped Chickadee

White-breasted Nuthatch

Tufted Titmouse

Evening Grosbeak

Towhee

Rose-breasted Grosbeak

Red Crossbill

Flicker

Redstart

Starling

Grackle

Red-winged Blackbird

Hairy Woodpecker

Yellow-bellied Sapsucker

Barn Swallow

Baltimore Oriole

Worm-eating Warbler

Black-and-white Warbler

Cowbird

Mockingbird

Mourning Dove

*   *   *

Frozen mice are kept in the Audubon Center's refrigerator in order to feed the owls.

*   *   *

I am a good field naturalist. I do know the names. But more and more I have been influenced by Zen Buddhist attitudes. What matters is the thing in itself, the intrinsic esthetic experience of seeing *a* flower, or *a* bird in a certain position, in a certain light—rather than bringing out your book and saying, "Ah yes, a golden-crested cardinal."

JOHN FOWLES

*   *   *

"It's become a busy town. We loved the time when we'd be awakened by a rooster in the morning. It was so quiet on the highway, we could hear the tinkling of a piano from across the road on Sunday mornings. Now I don't think there's a rooster crowing anywhere in the neighborhood."

*   *   *

STAGE MANAGER: There are a hundred and twenty-five horses in Grover's Corners this minute I'm talking to you. State Inspector was in here yesterday. And now they're bringing in these auto-mo-biles, the best thing to do is to just stay home. Why, I can remember when a dog could go to sleep all day in the middle of Main Street and nothing come along to disturb him.

THORNTON WILDER, *Our Town*

• • •

"Our house is on the highway, and we can tell, from year to year, how the traffic builds up. We're getting more cars all the time. It isn't so bad in the winter, but it's just terrible on summer weekends. We just stay home after church. We don't venture out. Too much traffic. You can see it building up late Friday—people coming up from the city—and then the flood back to the city Sunday evening."

• • •

Weekenders, as they are called by the basic townspeople, are city folk who live in the town on weekends (though not necessarily throughout the year) and holidays. They lead a double life—and pay double taxes—as they shuttle between a city apartment and their country house, preferably a quaint, old and authentically New England home, or something daringly modern hidden deep in the woods.

Often the couple or the whole family will make the Friday-evening journey to the country and the Sunday night trip back to the city. Or else, during the summer, the husband alone will do the traveling while wife or family stays here. In a number of cases the country house is considered the primary home: wife and children live here full time while the husband remains in the city most nights of the week. Some men stay in the city only two or three nights, and a few—I am thinking especially of an airline pilot—manage to spend a good deal of their time here. They are therefore much more involved in the everyday life of the town and more fully accepted as insiders. At the same time, a few old-timers have money enough to get away from the town for long stretches of time, particularly to Florida in the winter, whereas their forebears rarely ventured beyond our borders.

• • •

"Most weekenders are outside insiders. Or inside outsiders. Take your choice. You ought to hear the way some of them talk about 'townies,' taxes, schools and *outsiders.* No one is more anxious to keep outsiders outside than an inside outsider. Do you follow me?"

• • •

"You know Jim's place? Fellow named Winter had it first, and I remember the sign he put out in front: WHERE WINTER SPENDS THE SUMMER."

• • •

When an American says that he loves his country, he means not only that he loves the New England hills, the prairies glistening in the sun, the wide and rising plains, the great mountains, and the sea. He means that he loves an inner air, an inner light in which freedom lives and in which a man can draw the breath of self-respect.

ADLAI STEVENSON

• • •

Like most American towns, ours used to celebrate the Fourth of July in grand style, in fulfillment of John Adams' expectation that the adoption of the Declaration of Independence "will be celebrated by succeeding generations as the great anniversary festival. It ought to be commemorated as the day of deliverance by solemn acts of devotion to God Almighty. It ought to be solemnized with pomp and parade, with shows, games, sports, guns, bells, bonfires, and illuminations from one end of this continent to the other, from this time forward forevermore." In this spirit, the town was long accustomed to flying the flag, firing its guns, exploding firecrackers and ringing the church bells. (Because these bells served as fire alarms in the early days of our fire department, special action had to be taken to stop their haphazard ringing on the Fourth.) There were parades up and down Main Street and much oratory about the days of revolutionary fever when a town meeting voted to "heartily acquiesce in the wise and glorious effort for the preservation of liberty." Sixty-six men of the local militia served in the Boston and Long Island campaigns, and two companies rushed down the valley in 1777 to help fight off the redcoats. Most of the fighting and dying, of course, was done by the poor of the town instead of the men of property. The Indians sent 100 warriors, or a tenth of their tribe, to fight the British.

Despite the Independence Day tradition, the Fourth of July passes without much notice these days. Memorial Day has become the primary occasion for patriotic display, and the Fourth is seen as a glorious summer holiday, if the weather is agreeable, for basking in the sun or driving to a beach far from Main Street. Many citizens fly the flag, certainly, and the Sacred Heart country fair adds a festive touch, but fireworks are banned throughout the state, and patriotic oratory has gone out of style.

• • •

Twenty-five years ago Chard Powers Smith, writing about our river valley for the *Rivers of America* series, described it as "a region apart from the common restlessness of America. It has become a country where people stay."

Whether as a cause or as a result of its continuing pristine state, an impressive number of people have, from the earliest days, followed intellectual pursuits in the valley: theologians, political philosophers, miscellaneous writers, educators, scientists, artists and musicians who have come here to escape from the outer world's too insistent reminders of changeful time. Some have been born here, but more have immigrated in maturity, and many have been merely regular summer residents. The valley is less a cradle than a workshop for seekers of truth.

• • •

The warm weather not only brings us out of doors but ends our cultural hibernation. Just as the bare hills have blossomed, so we seem to be flowering ourselves. Up and down the valley we are feasting on a rich smorgasbord of the fine arts and the performing arts. Summer theater in drafty barns. Clothesline art shows on village greens. Concerts in sheds. String quartets on mountain estates. A solitary painter seen at his canvas in a field of bluebells.

In these backcountry towns, we had tucked ourselves away for the winter, sticking close to home and making good use of the time for what used to be called self-improvement. While icy winds rattled the storm windows and snow piled up against the doors, a good many of us—more than the rough cut of the countryside might suggest—read by the fireside, made music and tried our hand at painting, poetry and crafts.

The professionals among us were busy, as usual, through the long cold season. For many generations we have had in these hills a well-scattered colony of writers, artists, architects, actors, sculptors, composers, musicians, editors and scholars. Mark Van Doren writes his poetry on Cream Hill, in a town across the river, not far from the house where James Thurber lived. Lewis Mumford lives in the opposite direction. We can count as neighbors in nearby towns such interesting citizens as Arthur Miller, William Styron, Eric Sloane, Robert Osborn and Hal Borland, who has written the unsigned nature editorial in *The New York Times* every Sunday for nearly thirty years. Swing your arms wide enough and you are likely to strike a poet, magazine writer, book reviewer, mapmaker, cartoonist, folk singer or harpsichord maker.

It amounts to a well-spaced workshop of the arts and letters which carries on without pretension and preciousness, without even attracting much attention, because the creative people have rooted themselves deeply into the rural life. An illustrator serves as a selectman in one town. An actor raises Christmas trees. Established authors do some farming on the side. An artist serves on a Planning and Zoning Commission. Main Street merchants decorate their shops with their own works of art. One of our garage mechanics is a fine violinist. The artist who lives over on Treasure Hill draws the comic strip "Flash Gordon."

Altogether, it makes for a creative and appreciative atmosphere that is enhanced by the considerable number of citizens who are involved in education, one way or another. We consequently may enjoy a greater degree of tolerance of dissenting opinions or peculiar life-styles than one normally expects to find in a small town.

· · ·

"I honestly think you can do anything or say anything in this town and nobody's going to get too upset—except if you abuse the flag. That's something I wouldn't advise. Your war veterans especially, they feel they fought for the flag and they saw people die for the flag. It sums up everything they feel about the country. We've had one little incident here. Some kid, protesting something or other, burned the American flag in front of St. Andrew's. It was all over before it started, and it never blew up into anything. But one of our liberals, he told this kid he'd beat his head in if he ever saw him walking around at night."

· · ·

"You know, an artist has a great deal of trouble. If enough artists establish themselves in a place, then the rich people follow and the prices go up. That's what happened at Lyme, Woodstock, East Hampton, Provincetown, places like that. And sometimes, later on, the riffraff follow the rich. Well, here, a different thing occurred. Quite a few artists moved in after World War One. You could buy a place for a thousand dollars or less in those days and fix it up. But for some reason the wealth didn't follow. It never became the kind of artists' colony that made it fashionable for people to come in and build big houses. An architect friend of mine moved away because the houses going up were too small for him. Only very recently are we getting city people paying enormous prices for these old houses or putting up expensive houses so deep in the woods that you never see them."

· · ·

"The town has a marvelous range of architectural styles, a really valuable heritage. There are a number of prerevolutionary

Colonial houses with huge fireplaces and hand-hewn beams. Some
of them still exist because they were incorporated into the much
larger, stately houses of the Federal period, beginning around
1790. Then came the Classical or Greek Revival style from the
1830s until the Victorian period, when the houses along Main
Street were built. One Englishman said the house across from
the pharmacy was the finest example he had seen of the transition of Victorian architecture to America. So we have the full
range, from Colonial to modern, and one of our blessings is that
we didn't have wealthy people coming in here, as they did in
some towns, and changing the old houses so completely that
hardly anything of the Colonial period is left. The houses here
have been left alone, pretty much, and the new people moving
into town today have sense enough to leave them be."

• • •

The cultural dividing line between a city and a town is hard to define,
but I'd say a town is a place where if you see a kid with long hair, you
can assume it's a girl.

JAMES SIMON KUNEN, *The Strawberry Statement*

• • •

Not quite. Some of the town's long-haired kids are boys. The
longest hair I've seen locally was on the head of a carpenter's son
who graduated from high school last year. Our youngsters catch
on fast to the fashions of youth. Television teaches, for better
and worse. The town is off the beaten track and far enough from
any big city to keep the kids close to Main Street, but they are
not immune to the signals and temptations of urban America's
youth culture. Like all the towns hereabout, we have a local drug
problem. It is small, and the reaction so far of parents, children
and authorities has been calm and responsible. (Officials and
student leaders at the Regional High School have brought in
young addicts from a rehabilitation center to talk directly to students about drug abuse.) But most of us are appalled that drugs
should find their way here at all. Last year, when four young

drug users, one of them a 16-year-old girl, dynamited the high school's exterior and the vice-principal's office in the small hours of a foggy September morning, one could feel shivers running up and down the spine of the valley. In these little country towns we are all television voyeurs of other people's troubles, watching cities in riot and seeing distant reaches of the nation in turmoil. Suddenly we were a little less complacent, a bit more anxious.

•   •   •

Burning some trash behind the house and feeling guilty for being a polluter, I see a scrap of paper fall to the ground after a brief ascent in a plume of hot air. It is in Jan's handwriting, a 16-year-old's note to herself: "I think I am trying to comprehend the whole world at once. That is what is so exhausting."

•   •   •

A picture on the front page of a regional newspaper shows a pile of trash in one of the towns hereabouts. The caption explains:

Illicit defilement of the lofty beauty of Cathedral Pines was found by Frank Calhoun. Searching through the mess, he found a postcard which clue he turned over to the Nature Conservancy and the dumper was traced and apprehended. He was an 18-year-old local resident who, having been sent to the Town Dump with the trash, decided to save time by some impromptu dumping. He has been ordered to clean up his mess.

•   •   •

Our troubles with the young (and theirs with us) are minor and traditional, and the life they lead is straight, square and achingly familiar—echoing the days of another, easier-going America. Except for their greater awareness of the wider world, these small-town youngsters—at least many of them—seem to be much in the mold of their parents and grandparents. Although we worry about there not being enough work in the town to hold the younger generation, many of our youth will settle down here and live close to their relatives. "There's one thing you can still find in this town," I was told, "that's just about dead every place else in America. That's the old tradition of sons following in the footsteps of their fathers. Just count up how many father-and-son operations we have here."

* * *

When I asked a schoolteacher the other day about a boy who is said to be quite a troublemaker, she replied, "Well, I remember teaching his father. He was the same way. And his sister too!"

* * *

In those old prosperous days [of the mid-nineteenth century] there were many more houses at Bulls Bridge than there are now and during the winter term there were 60 pupils attending school. That was a hard school to discipline. The big rowdy boys had done their worst one winter and succeeded in making life so miserable for the kindly gentleman who was the teacher that he gave up his job. The district committee secured a strong, determined man to fill the vacancy, directing the new teacher to be the boss at whatever cost.

That teacher was known to lift big boys off the floor, holding them with head hanging down until they would beg for mercy. One especially unruly lad was taken to the hot-box stove and had his head stuck into the open stove door and held there until the scent of singeing hair was smelled around the room. Such strenuous punishment restored a degree of order in the school for the rest of the winter.

LAURA D. NEWTON, 1939

* * *

"When I went to school—that was a long time ago—there was one boy who was so bad they could never keep a teacher there for more than a few months. Then one little teacher came along, a tough Irish girl, and she asked Will Templeton, who was on the school board then, what she should do with this great big bully if he made trouble. He told her to hit him with anything you can get hold of. All right, she said. In those days the schoolhouse, like all the schoolhouses in the country, had a long stove that took a three-foot stick of wood in the fireplace. There'd be a stove poker on top. Well, she started teaching and this bully started in on her. She was walking up the aisle one particular day and he stuck his foot out. She went flat. That got her Irish up. She turned right around, grabbed that poker and gave him one right on the side of the head. She laid him cold! Right in the middle of the aisle! Passed right out! He finally got up, scared to death, and walked right out of school. He never came back again."

•   •   •

"Our eighth-graders, the ones who will be going on to high school, aren't half as mature as your city or suburban eighth-graders. They haven't learned the habits of getting along in larger groups. They don't know how to behave when they go into a roomful of 30 people and they only know two or three of them. So when they go up to the high school, which has some of the problems of the typical suburban high school, they're in a whole new world. Some of these kids have been terribly overprotected. They haven't gotten around too much. Suddenly they're confronted by a fantastic amount of things: What activities to choose? What sports? Dances right away in the ninth grade? How to use my time? Boom!"

•   •   •

"It's difficult for the kids to get together here. The houses are so scattered, and the parents, if they're able and willing, have to do a lot of driving. I think the Pilgrim Fellowship at the Congregational church is the only really active youth group in town, outside of the Boy Scouts and Girl Scouts. They even have some of the Catholic kids in it. The youth group at the Episcopal church is defunct. It would be wonderful if the three churches combined in this—have one youth group—but somehow it's hard to work out. There was some kind of open house for all the kids a few years ago, but there was trouble, not enough supervision, some things torn down. Then parents got upset because their kids were hanging around with some of the rotten apples. But something could be done. The three churches managed to get together for the Vacation Church School, and now everybody's proud of it. The kids get together for a couple of weeks early in the summer, take field trips, do arts and crafts, get some religious education. They even take in some fresh-air children up from the city. It works out fine."

• • •

We are particularly excited about our vacation Church School this year. We have an excellent teaching staff from all three Churches and a superb line-up of films on the theme "Living in God's World." Vacation Church School is quite different and a lot of fun. For three-year-olds through 8th grade. Cost: $2. per child, maximum $4. per family.

ANNOUNCEMENT

• • •

Youthful troublemaking today is seldom serious. Mostly pranks. Some vandalism, especially on Halloween. Some stealing, but it's hard to get away with it when so many parents feel some sense of responsibility for all the juveniles, not just their own. The necessary system of school buses, which pick up the children immediately after classes or sporting events and transport them home, effectively eliminates any hanging about after school. We have very little in the way of a street-corner society even though there are a few regular truants. Teen-agers outside the village have a major problem getting together with one another after school.

For the most part, the pleasures of growing up here are innocent: winter sledding parties, summer swimming at Emery Park, Little League baseball, year-round games and adventures. There are "Pee Wee" and "Squirt Bomber" hockey teams, the Scouts and Explorers, the Pilgrim Fellowship. In the spring, girls as well as boys take a softball glove to school with their books and lunch bags. There are homework, dishes and chores to do, and money to be made baby-sitting and cutting lawns. Farmers' sons drive tractors and hay wagons. But for the most part the pressures are light. The children of the town are allowed their time in life to be young and carefree. They may emerge from their teens a little less sophisticated than their city and suburban counterparts, but they will have enjoyed an almost classic kind of childhood.

• • •

"You have to make a distinction between families which are really active and doing lots of things and those that just plod along. The biggest problem with the kids here who get into trouble or have real problems is that they wake up in the morning and don't have anything to do. There's no reason to get up. They go to school, but that's it—they have no interest in the school and no interest in anything else. They have no sport after school, because they forgot to sign the paper or something. You ask them what they're looking forward to, and it's like a complete void."

• • •

Memories should endure. Unless we know where we came from, something about the road we traveled as a people, how can we know who we are and where we are going?

HAL BORLAND

• • •

A good day to be reading *Kirby Benedict*, a biography by Aurora Hunt of a legal associate of young Abe Lincoln who later became a colorful federal judge in the Southwest during the frontier days. He was born in this town in 1810, the youngest of eight children of John and Chloë Benedict. He grew up in a bucolic atmosphere which is not unfamiliar to our own youngsters.

His boyhood passed uneventfully in the quiet village. . . . There were fish to be caught in the river as it rippled its summer waters and winter cataracts through the valley that lay green and serene between the bordering hills. Chestnuts ripened in the fall when the maple trees flashed their splendor and Mount Algo offered her gentle slopes for young legs to climb.

The elementary schools . . . provided ample opportunities for young Kirby as they were in session nearly the entire year. Male instructors were employed during the winter, but in the summer the women assumed that duty while the men harvested the wheat, rye, Indian corn, flax, and buckwheat or repaired the chestnut rail fences and the bridges that had been damaged by the winter storms. . . .

• • •

During those same early-nineteenth-century days, a distinguished local lawyer, Barzillai Slosson, wrote a brief history of the young town. He described the way the river, coming down from Massachusetts, twists and turns as it passes through the town, racing through the narrows, idling in the broad passages, finally rushing "with great violence down a rocky steep for a considerable distance. In times of high water it forms a scene truly sublime. The water falls about 70 feet in a distance of about 20 rods. The place is known by the name of Bulls Falls. A bridge is thrown over the narrowest part and affords a safe and delightful view of the cataract."

Today the stretch of river from our metal bridge to the old covered bridge, and to the small hydroelectric plant nearby, still offers views both sublime and delightful. Here a little island that serves as a nursery for deer; there a solitary fisherman under a straw hat; over there a cabin by the water's edge, scarcely visible in the thick vegetation along the shore; in the distance, schoolboys practicing for a crew race, their long oars propelling a graceful shell. On one side of the river, there are a few houses, barns, cornfields, and cars traveling along the highway. On the other side, Schaghticoke, the largest of the four remaining Indian reservations in the state. Only a dozen middle-aged and elderly In-

dians still dwell on these tax-free government-maintained preserves, and for many years now only a single Indian has lived on
the 400 wooded acres of Schaghticoke.

* * *

"We people who lived in the Bulls Bridge school district grew
up with the children from the reservation and looked upon them
the same as other neighbors and friends. It was a common thing
to see a group of the older Indians going along the road in various directions loaded down with baskets of all descriptions—from
strong oak bushel baskets, which the farmers liked to own when
picking corn or digging potatoes, down to nice little ones made
from very fine black ash splints."

* * *

"There was one old Indian on the reservation, some years ago,
who had terrible rheumatism in the knees. He had to hobble
about with a cane. One day he struggled painfully down the
cellar stairs of his old house to get butter from a crock. When
he spied a rattlesnake coiled up on the floor, he dropped his cane
and bolted up the stairs in record time. It cured his rheumatism,
just like that! He never suffered pain in his knees again."

* * *

The name Schaghticoke, wrote Slosson, "was originally applied by the Indians to a large brook and signifies in their tongue
long brook." He noted that "the present number of Indians is
about 40. They are the descendants of the remnant of the Pe-
quods who escaped the destruction in the swamp at Fairfield in
the year 1637. The old persons among them relate the transactions of that memorable day as they have been handed down by
tradition. . . . Their settlement [in our town] preceded that of
the English by 12 or 14 years . . . at that time the Indians could
muster 100 fighting men. . . . They were an industrious people
and cultivated their lands so as to obtain a comfortable subsist-

ence. They owned horses and cattle. Considerable pains were
taken to instruct them in the Christian religion but the success
was not answerable to the expectations of the settlers. . . . While
any portion of industry remained among the Indians they were
enabled to raise a sufficiency of corn for their own consumption
and lived in a state removed from want. But a habit of extreme
idleness and intoxication has long prevailed amongst them and
almost without exception their lands have remained uncultivated."

•   •   •

The Indians improved daily and wonderfully by their intercourse with
the whites. They took to drinking rum, and making bargains. They
learned to cheat, to lie, to swear, to gamble, to quarrel, to cut each
other's throats, in short to excel in all the accomplishments that had
originally marked the superiority of their Christian visitors.

WASHINGTON IRVING

•   •   •

Schaghticoke today is silent, shadowy and almost eerie in its
atmospheric suggestion of a lost culture. Aside from the rare car
raising dust on the narrow river road, and apart from the birds
and little animals scurrying about the forest, it is a timeless, mossy,
moccasin-quiet retreat. Still standing in near ruin is the little stone
mission house of the Moravians who worked among the Indians
in the early decades of the eighteenth century. Birds nest in its
tiny bell tower; the skeleton of a fish is carved on a wall. Farther
along the road, in the Indian burial ground, there are crude rocks
and simple headstones marking the dead. One says of Julias
Scicket, who died in 1885 at age 29, "Youth forward skips, Death
soon it nips." Another reveals the long, long life of "Eunice
Mauwee, a Christian Indian Princess, 1756–1860." Her father was
a chief who became the first of the Schaghticokes to be baptized
by the Moravians. He must have seen the arrival of the first
white settlers.

• • •

Way back in 1719, to make sure that there would be an orderly settlement of this frontier area, the Connecticut General Assembly decreed that there would be no trespassing until surveys had been made and a procedure established for the creation of townships and distribution of land. The Indians had been persuaded to give up the territory for a few pennies per acre. Our town, originally twice the size it is today, was sold at an auction in the Windham courthouse in March, 1738. Fifty shares were purchased for about 1,200 pounds, and three other portions were set aside for the support of the church, the schools and the first ordained minister. Thus each shareholder or proprietor had a claim to one fifty-third of the new township. Most of the original proprietors were land speculators who soon profitably sold their holdings to genuine settlers. Even the settler proprietors made money selling off pieces of their land.

It was rough country that they had purchased, sight unseen. Ezra Stiles, an early settler in the next town up the river, wrote that "nature, out of her boundless store, threw rocks together and did no more." The pioneers who struggled through the first hard years in the wilderness, beginning with 40 families in 1738, were not humble or exploited country folk happy to scratch out a simple living but "versatile and ambitious men who sought economic opportunity in the new town." The late scholar Charles S. Grant, who wrote an excellent history of the early decades, concluded that the average inhabitant "does not appear to have been content with a subsistence way of life ('the happy yeoman'). On the contrary, one is impressed with his almost frantic pursuit of a wide variety of schemes or projects. One also notes a curious moral attitude, a combination of self-righteousness and a propensity for cunning deceit."

The town was incorporated in October, 1739, and the first town meeting was held the following December, at two in the afternoon on the fourth day. Abel Wright was chosen moderator. It was voted that Ebenezer Barnum, Azariah Pratt, Timothy

Hatch, John Porter and Abel Wright serve as selectmen for the year ensuing. Altogether, more than two dozen officers were elected. The town needed highway surveyors, fence viewers, constables and tithingmen as well as a town clerk, a treasurer, a leather sealer, a brander of horses, and other functionaries. Among many things decided at the first town meeting, the voters (eligible male adults) agreed to tax themselves for the support of the ministry, to allow swine to roam freely about the village, and to use as the community sign post "a black oak tree that stands highest to Mr. Joshua Barnum's house."

• • •

"The town progressed at an alarming rate" in its early years, according to one account. The land was "subdued," properties were fenced, orchards planted, rushing waters harnessed for power. Schools and a church and a meetinghouse were swiftly built. Dozens of roads were laid out, and the river was bridged. Daniel Comstock's general store and Ebenezer Barnum's sawmill and gristmill were followed by so many craft and commercial enterprises that the town was soon humming with activity. There were mills of every kind, stores and taverns, stills and tanneries, dyehouses and blacksmith shops, ironworks and potash works. And coopers, carpenters, cabinetmakers, tailors, shoemakers and jacks of all trades.

Half of the original adult male settlers became part owners of works, mills or shops. It was a thriving, throbbing frontier town: a farming-trading-manufacturing center in the lap of hills where there were wildcats and rattlesnakes to worry about and Indians to pacify. There were houses to be built, forests to be cut, crops to be planted, drovers and teamsters to be fed and put up for the night, things to be made and sold, children to be schooled, God to be praised.

• • •

A few years after the final inrush of immigration which began in 1761, the over-all picture of the valley was that of a region whose population was almost exclusively rural, and which approximated in size the rural population of the same region today. The Connecticut census of 1774 and the Massachusetts one of 1776 show that, agriculturally speaking, the land had already reached its saturation point. The chief difference from the modern scene lay in the fact that many of the hilltops which are now deserted were still under cultivation in 1760, whereas many of the valleys where the best farms are today were then still swampy, miasmic, infested with bears and occasional wolves.

CHARD POWERS SMITH

•   •   •

By 1756 there were as many as 1,000 inhabitants in the town. The number doubled in the next two decades. The townspeople wondered how the place could survive such a population explosion. The Revolutionary War solved the problem. According to a brief local history written by the late Ann Hopson, "tales of growing oppression of the British inflamed the restless ambitions of the young men of the second generation, who were perhaps less enamored of the back-breaking and endless rocks of the beloved 'rocks and rills' of their fathers. They could not share the gratified sense of achievement of their parents. The declaration of war offered them their opportunity. Many young men left the town and some of them did not come back. A few were left on the battlefield probably and some, after hasty farewells to their families, pushed on to the west—Pennsylvania, New York State, Ohio, the new wilderness."

All of these filled-up hill towns contributed to the extraordinary westward migration from New England—half a million by 1860—described by Stewart Holbrook in *The Yankee Exodus*. The townspeople who remained and prospered erected many of the handsome white farmhouses and red barns that grace our slopes and plains today. Those of us who live in these lovingly made homes, gathering logs for the same stone fireplaces, storing our hay in the same fragrant lofts, mending the same stone walls, worshiping in the same churches, going by the same town-meet-

ing rules, feel close to those good times. We are sustained by a
sure sense of continuity.

• • •

They were a nicely named people, those early settlers. Reading
the early church registers, one glimpses poetry in such names as
Delight Morgan, Wealthy Randal, Patience Dye, Thankful
Berry, Zeruiah Thankful, Salome North, Electa Bradshaw, Fear
Hubble, Sarah Converse, Lydia Skeel, Eleazer Lacy, Disa Brown,
Salmon Douglas and Mindwell Parish.

• • •

The town had furnished some 150 men for the Revolutionary
War and nearly the same number for the Civil War. But few
came home alive or intact. At Cold Harbor, Virginia, on the first
of June, 1864, more than 400 men of our county, including many
local boys, died in battle. Our town lost more men in the Civil
War, in relation to its population, than any other in the state.

• • •

When it became too much of a nuisance to let the swine roam
about freely, there were those who took to cutting off the tails
and nailing them to fences for all to see. Part of the township became known as "Pigtail," and one enterprising local merchant
won national attention for labeling his store, stationery and containers with the slogan "Pigtail Against the World."

• • •

It has always been a place of farms, a home for farmers. Whatever else people did, this was above all a grain-growing, corn-
husking, hay-cutting, cattle-raising, chicken-feeding, horse-
breeding, milk-producing, tobacco-harvesting town. And we
still have manure on our boots. Some of our kids are Future
Farmers of America. One lady keeps on winning prizes for the
most productive cows in the territory. We enjoy the most bucolic of surroundings, almost as if the industrial revolution had

never happened. For much of the eighteenth century and most of the nineteenth century, however, this was also a smoky, gritty, iron-mining, iron-forging town: a mini-Pittsburgh. The whole of the region, which at one time had more than two dozen iron furnaces in operation, was a major production center for some of the finest grade ore in the world and for the tools of industry and war. The discovery of the Bessemer steel-making process, using low-grade ore, marked the beginning of the end of the small-town iron industries. Our own iron activity came to a dramatic halt in 1895 when the last important furnace was shut down and the adjoining river dam was blown up.

For many busy years these now-peaceful hills were aflame with charcoal fires. It took about 130 bushels of charcoal to smelt a ton of iron ore. There was a great din from the mines and chok-ing fumes from the furnaces. Ore-laden ox carts rumbled down the muddy highways, and it was not unusual—at least until the arrival of the railroad—to see nearly two dozen ox teams plodding in succession through the covered bridge, taking pig iron out of town to the ironworking industries. The population reached 2,000 during the height of the iron boom, and there may have been hundreds more transient workers on the scene. Two hun-dred men were employed at Bulls Bridge furnace (and 61 chil-dren were packed into the little district schoolhouse), where armor plates were produced for the ironclad vessels of the Civil War. In the heart of the township the principal iron company created a veritable company town. One settlement of working-men at the foot of Skiff Mountain was known as Alder City. Only a few filled-up and overgrown cellar holes remain today. Iron ore and pig iron were used as well as money in our local transactions, and many a worker, perhaps brand-new to Amer-ica, soon found himself deep in debt at the company store.

• • •

"A century ago all the grandfathers who ran the important businesses in the town would go down to the Battery in New York when the boats would come in from Europe, and they would meet people, the immigrants, and arrange to bring them up here to work in various capacities. Irish, Polish, Bohemians— that's how a number of families in town started. Many Catholics, of course. They came in, worked as iron miners or servants, stayed right on, married, bought land, worked on the tobacco, and built up their own establishments. Now they are old and respected families."

• • •

"There was a more clear-cut class structure in those days. The rich man in his mansion, the poor man in his humble home. It was the era of the live-in servant, but all that is gone now. You have to make do with ladies who clean by the hour, if you can find them. There's one woman who takes care of several families that way. She goes to Florida for the winter."

• • •

"For a long time the town had a huge business exporting ice. You wouldn't believe how much ice went down our roads. There were icehouses all around. When the right time came in the winter they'd hire all the men they could and start cutting ice like crazy—on the river, the ponds, wherever there was ice. They'd get it into the big icehouses and finally ship it down to the city for people to use in their iceboxes."

• • •

Once the iron era was played out, the town not only shriveled with the departure of many workers and their families but experienced a withering of its spirit. There was a loss of drive after so many decades of frenzied enterprise. "It was once a flourishing community," wrote Francis Atwater, a local historian, in 1897. "The charm of the town now lies in its quietness and solitude." The place seemed to go into semiretirement as one of the "old settled towns of New England." Main Street had matured into an attractive tree-lined thoroughfare, though still unpaved, and there were many fine residences all about with beautifully shaded grounds, but there was evidence too of deterioration. "The land which was once profitably tilled in this vicinity has gradually degenerated, and much that was formerly cultivated, is now either given up to pasture, or to woodland, or is wholly abandoned."

As the years rolled by, according to a memoir by one of our senior artists, families that had lived on the land for generations faded out completely, and the auctioneers were called in to dispose of the accumulation of several lifetimes.

The numerous auctions filled many a need indoors and out. They also made good entertainment available before the movies came into our section. As the auctioneers did not as yet have to be licensed, local men gave color to the sales because of their familiarity with the contents of the houses and the folks who were selling out. At one sale a trunk that received no bids was opened, and all the intimate concerns of a generation of mothers and infants were sold piece by piece amidst wild hilarity. If bidding lagged, the "lingarees," as the auctioneer called them, were thrown at one of the town's eligible bachelors, and ten cents charged up to him for each handful. Scarcely a week passed without a sale, and the chances were that ten cents to a dollar would buy almost anything.

The farmers who remained kept the town going. "We really lived on those milk checks," one old-timer remembers. "There were cows all over town and quite a few creameries. This has always been one of the most productive milk counties in the country." Tobacco provided a vital cash crop for many hard-pressed farmers. According to an old Skiff Mountain farmer, "If the tobacco plants were lucky enough to escape hailstorms and survive windstorm damage, a lot of patient work and loving care was rewarded by a good cash return. With luck, tobacco growing became a mortgage lifter."

• • •

There was an economic lift soon after the turn of the century when a power plant was built at the falls by the covered bridge. During construction some of our more religious townspeople provided a mission for the Italian workers living in a shantytown. There was a cultural lift too when the first of our boarding schools was started in an old farmhouse by a young Episcopal monk. Wearing a billowing white monastic habit with a broad flapping shoulder cowl, he was for nearly 50 years one of the most visible and admirable personalities in a village that knew no shortage of characters.

• • •

"When we first came here in the early 1920s there weren't any roads paved. It was all sand, mud and snowdrifts. There wasn't even a bridge in the middle of town, because the ice took it out the winter before. The bridge just rolled down the river after the big floes of ice, and the trees and everything knocked down the piers. We used to drive on the river in the wintertime if the ice was thick enough. If the road was too drifted we'd just go down the river in a horse and carriage, far as Bulls Bridge. The drifts were so bad after snowstorms that you couldn't get far in a car. You couldn't go north of town. But there weren't many cars anyway.

"And in the spring the mud was just terrible. People today just don't realize how bad it was. And going up by your house, all those thank-you-ma'ams every once in a while, like waves in the road. There were places in town you couldn't get to in the winter because of the snow and in the summer on account of the mud. It was quite a problem. People had to walk or wait for it to dry out."

• • •

"First car I ever rode in was an E.M.F. That's what we used to call 'em: Every Morning Fix."

• • •

Until World War II the town sort of poked along. People farmed or sold stuff to farmers. They operated inns and camps for summer visitors. Artists and retired professionals discovered the beauty of the place and moved in. Modern times brought some unsettling changes. The icehouses and creameries closed

down one by one, but the paved state road came through at
last, and power lines spread to distant reaches of the township.
Tractors replaced workhorses, trucks replaced wagons, and more
and more people acquired telephones and automobiles. The general living standard increased, but the population decreased until
it came close to slipping below 1,000 at the beginning of the Depression. But then it began to rise again, beginning with those
returning native sons who decided that home was preferable to
the city during hard times.

• • •

"You can't say that we were hurt too much by the Depression.
There was plenty of common labor for fellows who weren't too
proud to work. One big-city executive came to our store asking
for any kind of a job. We put him to work at $20 a week sweep-
ing out the store. He was one of those who didn't jump out of a
window."

• • •

The figures show that this has been an up-and-down but
never-going-to-extremes town, oscillating between one and two
thousand inhabitants during the two-century leap of America's
population from under 4 million to more than 200 million.

1739 — 440	1870 — 1,744
1756 — 1,000	1880 — 1,622
1774 — 1,996	1890 — 1,383
1782 — 1,883	1900 — 1,220
1790 — 1,318	1910 — 1,122
1800 — 1,607	1920 — 1,086
1810 — 1,794	1930 — 1,054
1820 — 1,956	1940 — 1,245
1830 — 2,001	1950 — 1,392
1840 — 1,759	1960 — 1,686
1850 — 1,848	1970 — 2,000
1860 — 1,855	

• • •

Things picked up considerably during World War II. Suddenly there was a demand for labor. Young men went off to battle. Civil defense was organized. An inventory of the town's assets was taken, and plans were made to take in refugees in case of attack or invasion. Aircraft spotters on a tall watchtower took turns scanning the sky in the unlikely event that a German or Japanese bomber should pass by. (During World War I a week-long scare shook the town. It was rumored that German secret agents perched on one of our mountaintops were using a powerful searchlight to signal enemy submarines off the Atlantic coast —at least 75 miles away.)

In the postwar period the town has flourished along with the rest of the country, and in most respects the average man's standard of living has improved dramatically. There are more cars and household appliances, more people going off on expensive vacations, more youngsters going on to higher education, more leisure time, better schools, better medical care.

Today this is a spruced-up, well-kept and comfortable old shoe of a town. On any of these drowsy summer days it may look like it is sleepwalking through the twentieth century, but in its casual modern dress it is alive and well, quietly going about its business and taking care to assure that the future will be beneficial. Our older citizens may speak nostalgically about "the good old days" but they do not insist that they were better times. The past is viewed with affection, but the present suits them. A healthy quantity of Yankee individualism remains after many generations, but the townspeople have shown their capacity to cooperate for the common good. New enterprises have been brought in without offense to the pastoral surroundings. A sensible zoning code, untainted by any excessive desire for exclusivity, was adopted well ahead of some neighboring towns. Special areas are set aside for business development, and the rest is one-acre residential and open space. The general concern for the preservation of the town's most precious assets for the benefit of all is an echo of the day in 1748 when Nat Slosson and Sam Canfield were appointed a committee of two "to take care of the woods on the common and see it is not destroyed by anybody cutting it off."

* * *

A fierce electrical storm, this July night. We have lightning conductors all about, but we are still shaken by memories of our fire last year, and the time, during another electrical storm, when white flashes came skipping down the staircase. We pull the switch to turn off all the power and eat by candlelight. The frenzied sky gives us a magnificent fireworks display, and then the rain comes crashing down.

* * *

That fire was our real introduction to the town. We had moved in the previous summer, but we had yet to discover the underlying clockwork of the community. Then one foggy January night, while sitting at dinner, we saw the reflection of flames on the drifts of snow behind the house. It was a fire in the furnace room, started by faulty wiring. We quickly telephoned the fire department, four miles down the mountain, and tried in vain to stop the flames, which were already sweeping up the staircase in the wing of the house.

And then the town came to our rescue.

A few days later I wrote a thank-you letter to the newspaper:

Those of us who live in these hills know that we need only step outdoors or drive a few minutes up the road to find the solitude, the spacious silence of woods and fields, which is denied to so much of mankind in an overcrowded, industrial world.

Where we live, on Skiff Mountain, it is possible on a cold winter's night to stand before the old farmhouse or walk through the pastures and see not a thing in the world but the silhouette of trees and soft mountains, and see not a light in the universe but the distant stars. It is beautiful and breathtaking. But if in such dark privacy you find yourself standing in the snow with your hastily clothed and frightened family, watching your home go up in flames, it is quite another story.

Suddenly solitude is oppressive. You have done your best but the fire is doing its worst, and you are helpless. You long for the sight of other human faces and helping hands. In such a situation it is heart-warming beyond belief to see in the blackness the first pinpoints of automobile lights and then the bright beams of a rescuing host of cars and firetrucks roaring up the hill and swinging into your driveway.

And then everything happens at once: volunteer firemen swarming about the house, friends running with lengths of hose, strangers don-ning oxygen masks, shadows chopping through the ice in the pool, the First Selectman going up a ladder, shopkeepers and artisans and workingmen disappearing into the smoke, neighbors hauling furniture and valuables out of the house and into the barn, people risking their lives for you.

It is as dramatic and emotional an experience as you have ever known, but later on, when it is all over, you take care not to over-dramatize. It had certainly been a serious fire but the older and greater part of the house had been saved, thanks to the alertness and efficiency of the volunteers. Except for the fireman who took in too much smoke, no one was hurt. Many other people had undergone far more tragic experiences. In fact, considering how much worse it could have been, you count yourself lucky.

And yet, for all that, it happened to you, and there were some things about the fire which keep spinning through your mind. The way the volunteers went after the flames, not by wildly smashing away with their axes but by containing the fire with the kind of skill and co-ordination which would seem to be beyond the abilities of a part-time force. The way one unknown fireman carefully put a sheet of paper on an antique chair before climbing into the attic. The person who said, when the fire was at its height, "You'd better get hold of your insurance man first thing in the morning," and your wife's reply: "See that guy going through the hole in the roof? That's our insur-ance man!"

The realization that in its own miraculous way the fabric of the com-munity had pulled itself together, instantly and instinctively, to assist a single family in trouble. (And not just this town. Neighboring fire departments had responded too, either by sending assistance or standing by to help.) The woman who had taken your wife's emergency telephone call had not only set off the firehouse siren but had signaled a network of housewives who called homes throughout the community to make sure the fire fighters would know where to go. Men at dinner, or in the shower, or out visiting in their good clothes, had raced up the mountain to soak themselves in cold water and choke in the fumes of a burning home. Yet hours after the fire was over they were still on the scene, throwing out debris, pumping out water, working on the furnace and electricity, and preparing to stay through the night to make sure that the last spark was out.

And the fact that dozens of townspeople, particularly the carpenters, electricians, painters and plumbers, knew the house as intimately as yourself. They knew where to go, and where the fire would go. Afterwards, a carpenter, beginning repair work on the roof, took a close look and said, "I put on these shingles." The house had been a part of the town for more than a century and a half. "It's a beautiful old place," a garageman said, "it means a lot to us."

And the people who offered you their beds and cars, the use of their washing machines, and everything else from clothing to the Pill. The neighbors who turned up with pots of soup and hot casseroles, and the grocer who told a friend, "I didn't know they had so many children and animals. I'd better send them some food." He did too—even food for the gerbils.

It is almost too much to bear: not the fire but the kindness. The involvement. The sheer humanity of it all. This is not what modern man is used to. The drift of the world is to the de-personalized city where the knack of survival is not to get involved. Avoid thy neighbor.

Our own route to this corner of New England has been through a series of great cities. We are now in these hills to stay, only hoping that they will stay as they are, at least for a while. For there is something so genuine here, so evocative of the pioneer spirit, that it is too precious to be taken for granted.

It is said that man cannot gain the future without losing the past. The future is fine, we say, but, please—not yet.

•   •   •

It is a plain, white-clapboarded, green-shuttered old farmhouse, said to have been built around 1810, in the days of Napoleon, the War of 1812 and the administration of James Madison, the fourth President of the United States. The simple original structure, with its two low-ceilinged stories above a stone-walled root cellar, and its thick chestnut beams and wide hand-cut floorboards, has been so much added to that there are now four fireplaces, six exterior doors and 60 windows.

After having been hearth and home for many families over such a long span of years, the house has acquired a quirky personality all its own. It hits back if you neglect to duck your head on the way from the kitchen to the mudroom. In the older rooms no lines are plumb and the floors tilt just enough to prove that the house has settled here a long time. It creaks and shivers but holds steady in the blizzards and windstorms. An electric pump in the cellar, drawing water from a well of unknown depth, squeaks and gurgles its own working song. The house has a lived-in look that forbids formality and makes it a haven and a playhouse, full of odd-shaped rooms, eccentric passageways and hiding places for children and other living things. The dog and the cat have space enough to coexist. Six gerbils live in a bathroom. A mouse inhabits the attic. Chipmunks disappear into the wall beside the greenhouse. Squirrels share the feeders with robins and cardinals. The children sleep in rooms with sloping ceilings. They pop corn in the fireplace, bottle root beer in the kitchen, bring home freshly picked blueberries and blackberries and eat the tomatoes and cucumbers they have grown themselves. Summer breezes blowing through the house bring us the fragrance of sun-warmed hay.

•   •   •

We decided to live here about five minutes after first setting eyes on the place one luminous July day. The house is nestled just below the brow of a gentle rise close to the top of Skiff Mountain. The verandahs on the southern and western sides look out upon maples and willows, stone walls and split-rail fences, pastures that run down to a brook, and a great expanse of dark woods and distant hills. On the other sides the view is of green lawns, apple trees, a red barn and a white stone silo, and of shimmering hayfields reaching to a deer run of tall evergreens, to a waterfall hidden in the woods, to a stream and a swamp and a forest that plunges down the mountain to the river.

A giant sugar maple, said to be one of the largest in New England, stands before the house like a guardian angel, lightning rod in hand. It creaks its ice-coated branches in the winter, explodes with green finery in the spring, manufactures cool shade in the summer and shamelessly shows off in the fall with bursts of red and orange leaves until releasing a final golden shower.

Beyond the sugar maple the barn repeats the story of the house. The original hand-hewn structure has been much added to over the years and has gone through numerous changes of life. The immense chestnut beams in the hayloft were notched and pegged by settlers who built things to last. The property has passed through many hands, and there are signs all about of former owners and ways of life—a well deep in the woods, an abandoned charcoal pit, the rusting remains of farm machinery, and crumbling stone walls in second-growth woods. A neighbor recalls that her grandfather built our silo. Someone else says that Peter Pratt used to race horses on the flat just beyond our evergreens. An old-timer remembers his boyhood days here—coon hunting, chasing jackrabbits, sawing ice on the ponds, hauling milk down to the creamery, going to the little red schoolhouse that still stands near the old Skiff house. This house was smaller then and the grounds were cluttered with all the sheds, pens and wagons of a genuine working farm.

· · ·

On various maps of the nineteenth century this is identified as the Soule place, but to present-day townspeople it is most often referred to as the Ladd place, even though the Ladds moved on more than a decade ago. "He was the fellow who raised a lot of chickens. If you poke about behind the barn you'll hit some of the old chicken-coop foundations."

• • •

"I'm afraid you'll have to wait a long time before we get around to calling it the Connery place. Of course we all know you live there, but we always seem to be one or two families behind in the way we identify property. I guess you heard the story of the city man, let's call him Mr. Smith, who moved to a country town and bought a farm from a man named Jones. Smith moved in and settled down, but people kept on calling his place the Jones place. After 20 years of this he gave up in disgust and sold out to a man named Johnson. Not long after that he passed through town one day and asked somebody on Main Street how Mr. Johnson was getting along. 'Johnson?' said the local man. 'You mean the fellow up at the Smith place?'"

• • •

"Way back, when I grew up in your house, we were always getting and cutting the wood. We had five stoves—chunk stoves. We didn't have central heat then. All those wood stoves made quite a chore. You just kept on cutting wood."

• • •

"Was life hard in the old days? We didn't feel anything about it. Just went along with it. There was always something to do."

• • •

"These days you can drive right down the mountain in comfort on a paved road to get to the village, but in the old days the farmers went down the back way. I guess it's just a horse trail now. It was a steep dirt road which came out at the river where we used to have the old north bridge. On the other side there was a flag-stop railroad station and a general store, a creamery and an icehouse. People used to bring down their milk and haul back their feed. It was really a steep and slippery climb. A fellow named Ned Berry came over from Ireland. He worked for a farmer, and one of his first jobs was driving oxen up and down that hill with a drag harrow to soften up the snow and ice in the spring so that it would melt quicker and get down to dirt. When we had those bad floods in 1922 the bridge tore loose and went rolling down the river. For a while they put a cable across there so that the milk cans could be sent across and people could pull themselves over the water with a rope. But all of that's gone now."

• • •

This mountain is named after Nathan Skiff, a pioneer who arrived in the town in 1761 and purchased a large tract of land on the far side of the river. With only Indians for neighbors, he lived for five years in a log cabin while building a frame house with the date "1766" cut into a square chimney stone. The house, now painted red and surrounded by huge sugar maples, is occupied by his great-great-granddaughter. Her nearest neighbors, just up the narrow rolling road, are elderly brothers and sisters whose County Cork grandparents came to these parts in the 1850s. They prefer to live in the old style, raising much of their own food and depending on log fires and chunk stoves to see them through the freezing winters.

• • •

"Old Peter Skiff went up in an airplane for the first time in his life when he was a hundred years old, and when they brought him down he said it wasn't very exciting. He thought he was going to see the whole world but he didn't. He was quite a character. He'd work all day sowing oats or rye back and forth across the field. He'd go both ways so as to do a good job. And then he'd walk all the way down the mountain at night to go to a lodge meeting and then walk home later. He was a Mason. One night at the lodge they were passing around cigars and they offered him one. He said, no, he had a cigarette. So they said, 'We didn't know you smoked, Mr. Skiff,' and he said, 'Oh, yes, I've been smoking ever since I was 80.' "

•   •   •

Some summertime notes. We are eating outdoors most of the time these days under a ceiling of maple leaves. We churn our own ice cream on Sundays. The Skiff Mountain Farm family has been cutting and baling our hay and storing it in the barn. Yesterday we called on a retired farmer to look over his vegetable garden. We came home laden with beets, carrots, squash and lettuce, fresh from the ground. The world's mightiest sunflower has grown up beneath our bird feeder. We find frogs in the grass.

•   •   •

Maybe the nicest thing about the town—and the most old-fashioned—is the way those citizens long in years grow old so gracefully and so naturally continue to play valuable roles in the workings of the community. Not only are there some three-generation households, but there are grandparents and even great-grandparents serving most usefully in local government and in the church and social organizations. Retired people still earn money superintending the tool museum, looking after the maintenance of the library, playing the church organ and taking on jobs that fit their experience. By their presence they strengthen the roots of the young.

•   •   •

"Until 15 years ago we had our own telephone exchange in town, but now we're tied into a bigger system. It was in a little house on Elizabeth Street. Several local ladies took turns at the switchboard, day and night. It was a great convenience because you could always get hold of people, one way or the other. I remember there was a man in New York who was anxious to talk to me, but he couldn't get any answer. The operator told him to call back later and she'd let him know where I was. When he telephoned again she said I would be out of town until Tuesday because that's what it said on the note I had left in a milk bottle."

.   .   .

The Interstate Commerce Commission has given a reprieve of about four months to our passenger rail service. The Penn Central, having reduced the service to almost the vanishing point, and none too subtly, is arguing that there are too few customers to permit it to provide even a single weekend train. It is a story familiar to small communities all over the country. A citizens' movement to save and revive the trains is underway, hoping to hold the line until the day when the nation comes to its senses, gives up its blind worship of the private car and superhighway and revives mass public transportation.

.   .   .

"You won't believe this if you look at the railroad today, or what's left of it, but I remember well before World War One the express train that came through here had a diner and about two chair cars and 12 or 13 cars on the train, and it ran through town at about 60 miles per hour. How it made the curves I never found out.

"They had it made in those days. You could get anywhere in Connecticut by public conveyance. This state was laced with trolley lines, railroad lines. And they ran on time. My father told me that all the store deliveries came by freight. And the traveling salesmen took trunks and suitcases with them on the train. They'd stay in town at the hotels or inns. The inn where the library is now—you could step right into the train. If you look closely at the railroad station, which is now just a big gift shop, a place to buy birthday cards, you'll notice the doors with high foot-worn sills. You could step right into the train from the station. We've lost a lot since those days."

.   .   .

"A few years ago, before they stopped the daily passenger service, you could easily go to the nearest big town to shop or do whatever you had to do. If you didn't have a car or were too young or too old to drive, it was a way of getting out of town. There were kids who'd take the train to their music lessons, or they'd meet their friends there. A youngster could do some shopping on his own instead of waiting for his parents to drive him there. It was a great convenience for the family without a car, or with only one car, if the husband took it to work. The wife and kids weren't stuck here. But now there's no daily train, and there's only the one bus a day. Something's really wrong."

•   •   •

"You needn't think that we had good service on the trains. This has always been a poor line, in my opinion. The trains were often late, and the darn fool local stopped at every roadway, so that sometimes you wouldn't get home till midnight. I once had to wait four hours because a locomotive just fell apart on the tracks."

•   •   •

"We've had train wrecks from time to time. Once a train went straight into Hatch Pond. Two engines, loaded with coaches and carrying 500 kids from summer camps home to New York to start school. By the time the train came through here they had moved the kids to the back end to feed them. It was going like the devil. It whizzed around the curve by the icehouse and shot right into the lake. Three enginemen died. A brakeman lost his leg, half of it anyway. Not a kid was lost."

•   •   •

"The railroad used to run a husking-bee train up here from New York twice a year, starting in 1937. It was really a throw-back to the days when the townspeople really did husk corn. They'd go out and pull off the ears and bring 'em in and dump 'em on the barn floors. Then nights they'd go out with lanterns and invite the neighbors in and take the husks off. They'd throw the ears in the corner and grind 'em later. Once in a while they'd find a red ear, and sometimes they'd have a jug of cider hid in the pile.

"Fellow named Charlie Williams, passenger man for the railroad, got the idea of hauling people up here from New York for a husking bee. They'd bring up four or five hundred people, twice a year. Some kind of hillbilly band would go down to Grand Central and take some corn stalks and pumpkins. They'd fiddle there during the day, bring the people up in the late afternoon; then we'd feed 'em and send 'em back before midnight. The railroad would pay the Grange two dollars or a little more for each ticket they sold. Of course, it was a lot of work feeding them all. We used to get big 20-pound turkeys and cook 'em up. There'd be music, singing, dancing and husking. It was quite a thing.

"The first year the New York papers wrote us up and *Life* magazine sent some photographers. We came out in 'Life Goes to a Party.' One time I asked a fellow standing by the bonfire what he did in New York. He said, 'Gosh, I live in Kansas. I happened to be in New York, and I saw the ad. Why, I raise more corn and wheat than the whole state of Connecticut!' Another time there was a couple dancing there, and he fell dead with a heart attack. Some people came year after year. But a few years ago when the Pennsylvania Railroad took over the New Haven, that was the last we heard of it. The husking bee just dissolved."

• • •

As soon as the train arrived in the little dairy town the New Yorkers hustled to the Community Hall where they partook of the good things that some 30 Grange women had prepared for them. One hundred and fifty pounds of beef were prepared, "gigantian" quantities of escalloped potatoes and cabbage salad, also 100 pumpkin and apple pies and 100 gallons of sweet cider and coffee.

After supper the huskers went outside where 100 shucks of corn awaited them. They rushed down between the rows of corn, husking as they went, and the man who found a red ear could kiss the girl of his choice and likewise the girls could kiss the man of their choice. After the husking the crowd went inside where square sets were enjoyed until midnight when the 500 sleepy New Yorkers headed for their train.

When the Grange master was interviewed—Mr. John W. Chase—he simply said, "When two old maids berated me for letting so many city folks invade our town and disturb the peace, I said, 'Why, shucks, these people are just like us folks right here!' "

RADIO BROADCAST, 1937

•   •   •

WE'LL COME TO YOUR FIRE—
WILL YOU COME TO OUR CARNIVAL?
VOLUNTEER FIREMEN

•   •   •

These are sweltering, blistering days. The sky seems to be full of stored-up energy. Sudden thunderstorms come crashing down on us, knocking out the power lines and water pumps and washing out the dirt roads. Then the sun comes through like a blowtorch, and we run for the shade. Even so, the three-day firemen's fair, just south of the village on the flats, has attracted record crowds. This is the season, in almost all these country towns, for the pleasures of cotton candy, hot buttered corn on the cob, ferris wheels, thrill rides, raffles, fireworks, flea markets, hole-in-one golfing contests, games of skill and chance ("Dunk the Bathing Beauties") and special added attractions. Our special attraction this year was supposed to be a sky-diving exhibition, but the stormy weather called it off. The fire companies go from town to town competing against one another in old-fashioned musters to see which is the fastest fire-fighting outfit in the valley. A day-long horse show at our carnival gives the horse-riding youngsters a chance to show off their talents before friendly crowds in their own backyard. A good many out-of-towners come to the fair and help us finance the fire department, but it is very much a local affair, a formidable volunteer effort, which is certainly the town's biggest outing of the year.

• • •

"This is a first-class fair, but you should have seen the show we put on in 1929 when we raised the money for the Seagrave pumper. Listen! There's more talent buried in this town than you'd ever believe! You've just got to dig it out. We dug it out and put on a carnival that lasted four days, and we really cleaned up. We grossed something like $10,000! We worked, and I think we had 32 booths when we got through, and three circus tents and a dance platform 75 by 100 feet. Watson's loaned us all the lumber. We had 15 or 20 fire departments in here racing against each other. We even had an autogyro and a fellow who came down in a parachute. Nobody had ever seen anything like it.

"All this was just before the Crash. The next summer or maybe the one after that, we lined up another fair with sandwiches enough to feed 10,000 people. Franklin Delano Roosevelt was governor of New York State at the time, and he came over one day in a little bit of a Ford with a state trooper driving. I believe he made his first mention of running for the White House on the big meadow along the highway. But the day we had this thing, all over the country there was a big epidemic of polio, and word went out to people not to get into any gathering. So it cut our attendance to two or three thousand, whereas we had been ex-pecting 10,000. Nonetheless, we made a few thousand dollars out of it."

• • •

Once the city represented the rainbow's end to small-town youngsters. Thousands packed their bags and went looking for the pot of gold. Some people still think biggest is best. But the people of small-town America are out to disprove the theory . . . and to remedy past mis-takes that resulted in rural communities with too few economic and social opportunities. Today, "new towns" are emerging from country hamlets. And broadening rural horizons beckon America's growing population. We of our nation's nearly 1,000 rural electric systems are proud to lead the way. . . .

• • •

It takes us only two hours to get to one of the world's greatest cities. It has everything we lack—exciting crowds, exotic shops, famous restaurants, great theaters and museums. But most of us seldom bother to go to New York. Some older folks have not been there for years. Some teen-agers have yet to make the trip. In a better world the inhabitants of country towns would be eager to make periodic visits to the city to sample the range of delights that only a metropolis can offer. We would seek its cultural and sensual stimulation as eagerly as city dwellers reach for the natural refreshments of the country. Unhappily, however, we have come to think of New York as a place where you lock your car, watch your coat and hold on to your wallet. Visitors up from the city, who seem to see this town as a kind of haven in the storm, confirm the impression we have of the city as a concrete jungle of muggers and drug addicts, polluted air and seething ghettos, screeching subways and brutish crowds. We decide we are well out of it. But it is not something that gives us much cause for self-satisfaction. Someone has written that there is still a lot of land left in America to ruin. If the cities are allowed to become unfit for human habitation, the ruination of the countryside will proceed apace.

• • •

I believe our government will remain virtuous as long as there shall be vacant land in any part of America, but when we get piled one upon another in large cities, as in Europe, we shall become corrupt as in Europe and go to eating one another as they do.

THOMAS JEFFERSON

• • •

"I hate going to New York. You feel so anonymous. I got so that I was talking to waiters and waitresses just for company. You would find someone surly, throwing down the drinks and every-thing, but if you talked to them like a human being they would start behaving like human beings. We asked one girl if she was Irish, and from then on she was Miss Charming, wouldn't leave the table. She was real warm and friendly after shutting off her natural inclinations. We got the whole story, about her troubles, her sister's daughter on drugs, the needle, the whole bit."

•   •   •

"When I went to New York last week and looked at all the tall buildings I said to my wife, 'It's amazing that there aren't more suicides.' You're right in there like a sardine. You can't take a deep breath if you want one. And you can't get a clean one if you do get one."

•   •   •

August Sunday. High winds in the morning but a still, sunny afternoon. Friends come over to spend the afternoon with us. Children barefoot. We swim, play badminton and softball, drink vodka tonics, watch the sunset. We hold on to the magnificent day as if it will be the last. I light a kerosene lantern, and we sprawl on the lawn in the balmy twilight, sipping coffee and watching the world go dark.

•   •   •

Altamont, New York, population 1,500, is described in *The New York Times* under the headline "WAR BAFFLES AN UPSTATE VILLAGE SO MUCH ITS PEOPLE SAY LITTLE."

Altamont, pressed against the base of the Heidelberg Mountains near Albany, is like most rural hamlets in this upstate area—a series of shops and stores that serve an ever-diminishing farm community in the area and that is more and more a bedroom annex to a nearby city.

The future of the village—is it going to die or be swallowed up by some larger community?—and the character of its commerce—should the feed store cater more to the lawn-and-garden trade?—are sources of concern and discussion daily. The war in Vietnam is an international problem that only periodically intrudes.

*   *   *

"The frustration that I run into in dealing with many of these people is that they haven't got any other viewpoint than just the local viewpoint. They have only known this town, and who owns these shops and who lives in these houses, so that it is extremely isolated when you come down to it. They haven't got a broader picture of what is going on. And this stays in the family: the young people will go along with the same kind of thinking as their parents, whether they've been exposed to other ideas or change or anything else. Somehow there isn't an atmosphere of mobility. Even the ones who have been in service and seen the world, or who have worked somewhere else—they come back and close up. They don't want to know what's happening in the world, or why it's happening. I don't know whether it's a retreat back to this kind of thing, away from some of the things they've seen, or whether it's just that they've seen it and 'that's enough for me; things are fine here.' You can only get them to react when they find some of these things encroaching on them."

*   *   *

I was born just outside of Boston in 1895. There were two people in town who'd been to Europe and they had to give a talk about it every year because it was so extraordinary. I hardly knew anything outside of the town. I was even told that the people in the next town were pretty dangerous people.

R. BUCKMINSTER FULLER

*   *   *

We concentrate on the problems nearest at hand. A war in Asia or the Middle East, or the nation's continuing racial crisis, or the grave political and economic issues that inflame national passions—they are out of sight or out of mind. Or so it seems. Despite the vastly more powerful means of communication which now bring the world into our living rooms, there is little public discussion of the subjects that burn so brightly on the television tube. And all too often what one does hear only bears out an observation made by Wallace Nutting nearly half a century ago in his book *Connecticut Beautiful*: "Despite the spread of newspapers, there is no small contingent of the population without the stimulus of public opinion, and who fall back on their own narrow interpretation of life."

Yet it is just as obvious that we have in this town no small contingent of the population deeply concerned about and eager to be informed about the state of the world. The Milk Bar sells a great quantity of out-of-town newspapers, including 230 copies of the Sunday *New York Times*. The two principal churches, led by young, socially concerned ministers, provide a means for concerned townspeople to be involved in issues as remote from local experience as prison reform and inner-city poverty. Two youths are sponsored annually for a spell of volunteer work in poor areas of the Caribbean. A local family boards a foreign student for a year's study in the United States. The private schools bring in lecturers on international issues and invite the townspeople. The small-town view is expanded by those inhabitants whose work reaches beyond our four corners. One man spends half his time in Southeast Asia.

●   ●   ●

Our political thinking ranges from the far Right to the far Left. In fact, one of the country's best-known anti-Communist writers lives just down a mountain road from the weekend cottage of a lawyer who has a certain fame for defending Communists. But almost all of us fall into the spacious middle ground. Though it is basically a conservative country town, there is no want of liberal expression. Recent votes on the high school budget reveal that this town is decidedly unwilling to join others in the region in a meat-ax approach to the rising costs of secondary education. And we have been happily free of the kind of poisonous controversy— the superpatriots squared off against the "radicals"—which has lately scarred and divided other American communities. But should such an emotional issue come our way, we could, I believe, muster from Right, Left and center a sufficiency of voices of reason to damp down hysteria.

In the normal course of events, however, the town is more silent than outspoken on public issues. There is a notable reluctance on the part of most townspeople to speak out publicly, to expose themselves to criticism, to become involved in touchy subjects. It is generally left to a vocal few to carry on the vital debate of town interests. Only a tiny percentage of voters attend public meetings, including town meetings, and fewer still open their mouths. And yet there is no livelier local institution than the grapevine of private discourse.

•   •   •

"The real thing is, people are afraid to stick their necks out. They won't say what they think! A few people will always express their views even if it makes them enemies, but the rest are either shy or they hate to give offense or they don't have any views in the first place."

•   •   •

"There are some people in the fire district who have been fighting for zoning it, like the rest of the town, for years now, and there are others who have been fighting against it for years. You know where they stand. But as for the rest: they come to the meetings, and they just sit there on their fat behinds, not saying a word, just going along with the majority view. Bunch of sheep!"

•   •   •

Every now and then the town bridles, at least as an initial reaction, when it is confronted by the unfamiliar, by anything that threatens to suddenly upset the customary tempo of rural life. Two summers ago a local couple, strong on civil rights, offered the use of their house, barn and grounds for a fund-raising picnic for the National Association for the Advancement of Colored

People. The NAACP. Rumors swept the town about busloads of city blacks which would descend on this innocent place. Little comfort was found in the knowledge that the town, following the routine of most communities, carries $300,000 worth of insurance against riots and civil disorders. A busload of dark-skinned Americans did, in fact, arrive at Ore Hill for a day in the country. Many townspeople turned up as well. It was a champagne kind of day. Music, games, an auction, fine food and lazy talk at tables set under the trees. Much money was raised. A good time was had by all.

Last summer our three churches got together to sponsor an outdoor folk-music concert to raise money for interdenominational social work in the slums of a Connecticut city. A troupe of United Nations folk singers was engaged to sing in their national costumes. But, again, rumors raced through town. It was said that we were in for the kind of massive rock festival which had inundated the countryside near Woodstock, New York, with several hundred thousand long-haired youths. "Some people here just went haywire about Woodstock," one organizer told me. The Catholic Church backed out as a cosponsor. The major boarding school would not provide a playing field for the concert, or any other field; such an unpredictable event would conflict with the program of activities planned for visiting mothers of students. The grade school grounds were ruled out. In the end the performance was held in the school auditorium. A few hundred people turned up. The singers were excellent. Some money was raised. A good time was had by all.

· · ·

"I really have mixed feelings about this town. At least where we used to live you had people who really wanted things to change; they recognized problems and tried to handle them. Of course, I can understand some of it. In many ways we would be better off if we could stay as we are. It pains me to go back to the place where I grew up, because we used to have a real swimming hole and there were farms all around the town. Now the farms

are full of housing. A friend of mine said the other day that he
was sorry his own son couldn't enjoy the simpler America that
he had enjoyed. But the trouble here is that we have so many people who just don't want to know. They resist anything new. They
don't want to hear about it. Look at the resistance to expanding
the grade school even though it was perfectly obvious that it had
to be done and that we could do it less expensively sooner than
later. Look at the resistance to continuing the French language
program in the grade school or the difficulties our ministers run
into just trying out some innovations in the churches.

"What you see here, I think, are certain built-in typical-small-
town prejudices reinforced by some newer residents who have
fled from the horrors and discomforts of the city and don't want
to face the fact that we have a few problems of our own which
we ought to deal with. You can find people who admit that they
just wanted to get away from the blacks and that they don't want
them here! Well, that's a subject that really hasn't come to the
surface yet. When it does you'll learn a lot about the way people
think, good and bad."

• • •

Historical note. There must have been some slaves in town long
ago. When John Mills drowned in the river in 1759 while building a bridge, he left among his worldly goods a long list of "mov-
ables," including "a serving girl," valued at 40 pounds, and "a
serving boy," valued at 20 pounds. The girl, named Rose Negro,
went to his daughter, Jane, wife of the Reverend Joel Bordwell.

• • •

"I don't think you can generalize about racial feelings here. For
the most part, the subject never comes up. I wouldn't be surprised if there were some people here who had never met a black
person. Probably only a few could say that they had ever had a
real conversation with a Negro. While in their hearts they know
that a man's color shouldn't be held against him, their whole image of blacks is of rioters in cities and of people who are always

demanding something more. Since they have no firsthand experience with city slums, they tend to resent all these demands. They are sure that all it takes is more effort, more get-up-and-go; that if only the blacks would try harder, everything would be all right. They feel they want something for nothing, and they associate them with violence. Well, of course, I *am* generalizing, but I think these are pretty common attitudes."

• • •

Dialogue on Main Street:
"The interesting thing to me is that the colored people don't want to bend down, do the low jobs. They demand this and that, but they won't do the work."
"But they had the low jobs for hundreds of years. They want something better."
"Yes, but they don't make good at it. If they made themselves desirable, everything would be taken care of."
"You'd still have the color difference. No matter what they did, people would still try to put them down because of their color."
"Yes, but it doesn't make a difference if you've got a neighbor and he's a good neighbor and you like him and get along with him and he does his job and helps you out a little. Why sure you'd take him in! If they're good at baseball they're accepted as athletes. That's all they've got to do is make themselves desirable and stop rioting, which only increases the hatred."
"Well, the rioting may be bad, but it's made the rest of us notice them. If we were in their shoes we wouldn't put up with some of the things they have to put up with."
"It'll carry on for generations, I'm afraid. Of course, we don't know much about it here. I don't think there's a colored family in the whole town. When people hear that they kind of marvel at it."

• • •

It happens that we do not have a single Negro resident. There is a black antique dealer on Main Street who commutes from a nearby community, and for much of the year there are other blacks in town, though seldom seen. There are several workers, one housekeeper, some students at the boarding schools and a few ghetto children brought up from the city by local families for the fresh air of a country summer. But we are, to an embarrassing degree, an all-white community in a nation that has 22 million Negro citizens.

Possibly it is true, as one real estate man says, that individual dealers have politely discouraged black house-hunters, but by the nature of things it would not have made much difference. Historically this community, like so many other small settlements in New England and the northern stretches of rural America, has had little experience with nonwhites, with the exception of the Indians. According to the U.S. Census, our county, which has only 140,000 people, is 99 percent white. Our children go through grade school without any contact with black schoolmates. They meet only a few in high school. Most grown-ups in town have no contact with that vital tenth of the nation. Ours is not quite the all-American town we may imagine it to be.

•   •   •

September. Summer's end. Camps closing. Campers going. Cabins boarded up. Boats pulled up on shore. A kind of sadness comes in with the chilly end-of-summer breezes. Boys beginning to practice for the football season. Corn in the fields, crushed apples under the trees. Leaves losing their green, promising the bright colors of an autumn death. It seems to be raining a lot more now. Intoxicated by the change of seasons, I drive around the hills and find in the next town to the south, close to the river, a giant gnarled oak, spreading its ancient branches low and wide. And the sign:

UNDER THIS TREE
GENERAL GEORGE WASHINGTON
HELD COUNCIL WITH HIS STAFF
SEPT. 20, 1780

AUTUMN

LATE SEPTEMBER. After a succession of rainy, chilly days and cold nights, we took down the screens, stored the lawn furniture in the barn and put blankets on the beds. But now a heat wave has struck, and we have gone back to shorts, bare feet, lunch on the porch and iced drinks. The dog drags herself about and seeks a cool kitchen floor or the shady side of the house. Reports from Manhattan tell of the temperature going above 90 and of air conditioners causing another power shortage. People here speak of the weather as unbearable, but at least we are not trapped in crowded subways or traffic jams. We can dress lightly and perhaps knock off work early to make the most of the shade trees and swimming holes.

· · ·

Watchers of television commercials have often seen our waterfall, along with its spreading trees and the profile of the surrounding hills. It has been used in a number of commercials by promoters of a cigarette which "you can take out of the country."

When the film footage for these commercials was being shot, it was a period of relative drought. Very little water was coming over the falls. Obligingly, the Volunteer Fire Department brought a tank trunk to the upper level of the cascade and discharged enough water to fill the needs of the movie cameramen.

CHAMBER OF COMMERCE BOOKLET

· · ·

While I was standing in front of the A&P this morning, a stranger came strolling down Main Street and paused just long enough to say, "This looks like a real nice town. Quiet. Peaceful. I come from a town like this in New Hampshire, but it's changing so fast you wouldn't know it. Full of city people running away from it all. Terrible."

• • •

John Kenneth Galbraith commenting on the rural scene in southeastern Vermont: "We don't have farmers here any more, we have professional mowers."

• • •

We find the warm body of a sharp-toothed raccoon near the house, killed by our little Siamese cat. We inspect the vegetable garden and see that the deer have once again leaped over the fence to eat the corn. Leslie starts up the spin dryer, and we hear a terrible noise, as if nuts and bolts had come loose. But it is only sunflower seeds brought in through the exhaust pipe by our mudroom mice.

• • •

The children are going off to school again now that summer's over. They go gladly, it seems to me, though they might feel that they have to deny it. Children aren't *supposed* to like school, and there is a great deal being said these days, and rightly so, about the grim and stultifying conditions in vast numbers of American public schools. Once again our town is well off, for both our grade school and the Regional High School are human-sized and humane institutions where the learning process is carried on more agreeably, I believe, than in most schools in the land.

• • •

It is not possible to spend any prolonged period visiting public school classrooms without being appalled by the mutilation visible everywhere—mutilation of spontaneity, of joy in learning, of pleasure in creating, of sense of self. The public schools—those "killers of the dream," to appropriate a phrase of Lillian Smith's—are the kind of institutions one cannot really dislike until one gets to know them well. Because adults take the schools so much for granted, they fail to appreciate what grim, joyless places most American schools are, how oppressive and petty are the rules by which they are governed, how intellectually sterile and esthetically barren the atmosphere, what an appalling lack of civility obtains on the part of teachers and principals, what contempt they unconsciously display for children as children.

CHARLES E. SILBERMAN, *Crisis in the Classroom*

• • •

Not that our schools are notably unconventional or boldly experimental. Judging by appearances, they would fit almost anyone's image of the typical middle-American school in this day and age. It is a familiar scene: the low, sprawling red-brick Center School with its new cement-block protrusions; the pupils all in a row in brightly lit classrooms with green blackboards; the noisy cafeteria; the playing fields churning with boys at softball and girls at field hockey. And up the river the high school, a substantial two-story fieldstone building of the 1930s, recently enlarged, with a stately white-pillared entrance. It is a place of bustling corridors, blue jeans and miniskirts, band practice, drama rehearsals, bright students complaining about the boredom of it all, teachers striving to make tired old subjects relevant for the "now generation."

Familiar, all right, but not quite the schools we used to know. (At a recent local school-board meeting, a member remarked favorably on the way things were done "in the old days." The chairman quietly said, "These aren't the old days.") One senses an eagerness to change and improve, a groping for fresh ideas and new techniques. In the main, teachers are responsive and administrators alert to the individual needs and natures of their charges. The high school is led by an outgoing, athletic young principal who keeps a baseball glove handy in his office and likes

to take youngsters on geological rambles. It is an energetic place
that has its share of the "frills" that some older taxpayers complain about: modular scheduling (permitting variations in class
periods and class sizes), "resource centers," calculators, audio-
visual equipment, film strips, microfilmed magazines, recordings
of everything from Shakespeare to Pygmy folk music, a work-
study program, vocational-agricultural training, black studies
and visiting poets.

It is clearly an innovative school, trying to keep pace with the
times and coming to grips with contemporary problems. More
than a third of the graduates go on to a four-year college, and
almost all the rest enter two-year community colleges or seek
some form of additional education. Unfortunately the constantly
rising cost of education, even though it is good value for money,
has touched off a small but fierce resistance movement of taxpayers who have been demanding across-the-board cuts in school
spending. Of the six regional towns, including two communities
known for their moneyed families, ours has been the one most
willing to vote the funds for quality education. As property
taxes go up, however, we appear to be in for an annual pitched
battle over the high-school budget.

• • •

As for our own Center School, whose principal is a lean,
friendly Yankee from Mechanics Falls, Maine, it seems to be
reaching beyond the conventional procedures of the classroom
to ways of inspiring creativity: making sure there is no smother-
ing of enthusiasm or spontaneity, no killing of the dream. While
there are still some things to criticize, the school has an open-
hearted, mind-stretching environment with room enough for
open-classroom experiments and plenty of attention paid to children with special problems. Now, with new facilities being
added, there are some exciting prospects for greater use of films
and records, more musical instruction, a new research center and
a large library to replace "our overgrown telephone booth."
What most impresses is the good-natured atmosphere. Perhaps

this is only to be expected in a small town's small school, but in America of the 1970s it should not go unremarked.

•   •   •

"I can remember back in the 1930s, we had one softball bat and one softball for the grade school and high school combined. That was our athletic equipment."

•   •   •

"The trouble with education today, it's so fragmented. When we went to school we had reading, writing and arithmetic. Now the time the children spend on things that people of my age think are frivolous—well, it adds up to quite a bit of the school day. With all this money that's being spent on education, there's less intelligence. There's less common sense. It's been discarded in this modern age. We're producing a generation of educated fools."

•   •   •

"I'm a teacher who's a strong believer in good old grammar. I think you have to know and understand the subjunctive case and what a noun is, what a preposition does and the rest of it. I think it's vital."

•   •   •

Public schools shall be maintained in each town for at least 180 days of actual school session during each year. . . . In said schools shall be taught, by teachers legally qualified, reading; spelling; writing; English grammar; geography; arithmetic; United States, state and local history; the duties of citizenship, which shall include a study of the town, state and federal governments; hygiene, including the effects of alcohol and narcotics on health and character; physical and health education, including methods, as presented by the state board of education, to be employed in preventing and correcting bodily deficiency; instruction in the humane treatment and protection of animals and birds and their economic importance, such instruction, when practicable, to be correlated with work in reading, language, and nature study; and such other subjects as may be prescribed by the board of education.

CONNECTICUT STATE BOARD OF EDUCATION,
Laws Relating to Education

• • •

"This is a really good grade school. We have a good atmosphere among the teachers and between the teachers and the pupils. It's a lot better than some of the schools around here. You can feel the way things improve as the years go by. We do a lot more testing these days, for one thing, so that we can know what these kids are capable of and what their handicaps might be. The children are thinking a lot more for themselves. They're not just being taught. I know I can do a lot more with them than I ever could before. You can be more intellectually demanding. They come to school with better backgrounds. They are exposed to a lot more, through television and other things, and I think their parents, the young adults in town, are a lot more thoughtful and expressive than parents used to be. When the eighth grade graduates you can get some good, original speeches these days, instead of all the old platitudes about striving for success, and so on. They used to get commercial graduation speeches and memorize them!"

• • •

"I said to my class the other day that I would like some suggestions as to where I have failed—I'm not perfect, not by a long shot—and I said I wish you would just tell me how I could make it more interesting. Well, boy, they had some great ideas! There was one subject that they just wanted to wade in and find out all about in their own way, instead of my telling them what to write. It was their own suggestion and you could tell that they would really put their hearts into it."

• • •

Our nation is at present in the early stages of major changes in education, especially in terms of content, methods and objectives. The rate of change is steadily increasing with new innovations appearing daily. With this increase much of the knowledge accumulated is obsolete before the student can use it. We can no longer impose conventional information on students and hope that after four years they may go on to succeed in a highly complex world. Based on this premise, we are continuing to attempt to improve our curriculum in the areas of content, methods and objectives. We must teach people to learn and keep learning. Problem-solving skills and methods of inquiry must be developed, more individualization must be used in instruction and the acquisition of knowledge must be encouraged through greater student participation, laboratory approaches, and individual projects.

PRINCIPAL, REGIONAL HIGH SCHOOL

•   •   •

"In the old days all the children walked to school. It wasn't the school's business to get them there."

•   •   •

The school bus has been the undoing of the old school districts and the little red schoolhouses. These simple structures, several of which are now used as private homes, once served as neighborhood social centers. They even came in handy for funerals. For most of the town's history, each of the 14 districts was pretty much in charge of the elementary education of the children, with the town Board of Education carrying out inspections and seeing to it that state standards were met. The school year lasted eleven months, at least in the early days. Male teachers were hired for the winter, women for the summer. Often the teacher would "board round"—staying for a week or so in the home of each of the pupils—instead of putting up at one dwelling at the district's expense. School attendance would thin out considerably in the spring, when the older boys would help with the farm work. Small private schools were eventually founded to provide education above the grade school level, but these faded out with the start of high school teaching in the town. The district schools finally merged into a single grade school. (At first some pupils rode to school on horseback whenever the buses were unable to climb the worst of the muddy roads.) The local high school disappeared with the creation of the six-town Regional High School, the first in New England. Unfortunately our town lies the farthest away from the high school, and today our own children must take two buses, beginning with the Skiff Mountain bus at 7:05 in the morning, in order to get to school before 8:15. Although it is a long drive up the valley, there is possibly no more beautiful school-bus route in the country.

•   •   •

Two ladies of the town have set down their memories of the pains and pleasures of attending a little district schoolhouse in the early years of this century.

In those days of something like 1908 . . . we *all* walked. School hours were from 9 A.M. until 4 P.M. and in winter it was quite a cold hike. I still today picture us simple kids trying to step on our shadows as the sun rays were sinking behind those hills and eating pig nose apples, fallen from the neighbors' trees along the roadside. Where today in the Macedonia area are lovely little cottages built, were, in those days, some deserted house or a lone barn or shed and I, for one, lost a heartbeat in fear a tramp was either bedding down for the night or crawling out in the morning at 8:30. There were no phones to call your school mates on a cold frosty morning to say come to my house, my father's going to drive me to school, you may ride with us. Many mornings with either the snow creaking under the wheels of a wagon or sleighbells jingling, my father was tucking his children under the horse blankets, so afraid we might freeze, as the temperatures were sub-zero, and we must be at school a mile away (some children were still farther away) at 9 o'clock. Then arriving at the little wood-heated school room we gathered close to that old stove with our wraps still on until way toward noon hour. Also, let's give the teacher a thought for her work and care. I guess at times there has been 30 pupils crowded in that little school house. Although the children struggled with their education, at the end of the day they were never too tired, after filling wood-boxes and bringing in big chunks for the night plus farm chores, but what you could hear their laughter and glee under a big full moon, out with their home-made sleds (the boys called them their double rippers) coasting down the Fuller Mt. hills. Say, you of the Atomic Age: wouldn't you love just a little taste of those days?

. . . .

In 1923, my brother, sisters and myself were enrolled in this school and it was our very good fortune to have a truly wonderful teacher. She had to cope with all the elements that accompany a completely rural school. Each holiday she planned appropriate celebrations and at Christmas the whole community came to our play and party. That meant some coming off Fuller Mountain in horse drawn wagons, and seldom did cold winter stormy weather keep people away. The school bus was a two-seated wagon complete with top and side curtains, drawn by a good team of horses. When the road was too full of drifted snow by the regular way, they used the road through Miss Hopson's land and by her lake, as that route didn't seem to drift so badly. What a long hard trip that was, but a completely accepted part of living and learning.

• • •

The one-room schoolhouses were not given up without a struggle. Today, "busing," the transportation of children to out-of-neighborhood schools for the purpose of racial integration, is an emotional issue in many school districts throughout the country, but it is not an issue here. Several decades ago, however, transporting pupils to a single central school instead of letting them walk to a nearby schoolhouse was a radical idea that aroused fierce passions. Consolidating schools was condemned as inhuman, immoral, impractical and, of course, socialistic. Economic realities carried the day when the enrollment in some district schools dwindled to half a dozen children or less.

A last-ditch stand was made by one distinguished citizen, Jerome Judd, who appeared before the School Committee one August day in 1927 to denounce school centralization as "a crime and a calamity." The little schoolhouse, he said, ensures against "vile language, vile poetry and vile practices." A large central school exposes children to possible fire, disease and road accidents. A sick child would be deprived of his mother's love "till the bus goes back at 3 o'clock, and by that time, if he has pneumonia, you may need the undertaker." It is the tiny rural schools, he insisted, "that have made America great and produced great statesmen. These schools have turned out honest, hard-working, God-fearing men and women and produced only a very small percentage of evolutionists, false scientists, schemers, socialists, bolshevists, radicals and reds. . . . Centralization destroyed Rome and centralization can destroy the great United States."

•   •   •

A new struggle is now shaping up over proposals for the regionalization of the elementary schools of the six towns that now share the same high school. The old arguments for the preservation of home rule and local control of education are being heard again. The individuality of our single Central School is at stake. State-sponsored regionalization would not, at least in the foreseeable future, mean the elimination of each town's grade school and the busing of children to a large regional school. It would simply mean pooling the operations of the six schools for economic efficiency (common hiring of staff, purchasing of equipment) and educational standardization (so that freshmen entering the high school would have a common background and advantages). While we might get a better-quality education for the dollar, there are fears that we would be giving up to a distant bureaucracy too much of our local say-so about the education of our young. But in this, as in so many other matters, the state tantalizes us with talk of more aid if we cooperate and speaks of reducing its financial assistance if we do not. Instinctive feelings about local autonomy are shaken by the fast-rising costs of public school education, now about $800 annually per pupil for our town.

We have had no town meeting on the subject so far. We have just been following the work of study groups. Perhaps we will have to vote for regionalization next year, and then, as they say, the fur will fly.

•   •   •

Next Sunday: The deacons invite you to attend our after-church coffee hour and discuss our experiment of roping off the back pews. Come and express your feelings about this change.

THE FIRST CONGREGATIONAL CHURCH

•   •   •

"Our church could use some more people. It gets kind of empty when the children go out to Sunday school after the first half-hour."

•   •   •

A Sunday to remember! After church we discussed the thorny issue of roping off the back pews. Over at St. Andrew's, the Episcopalians, we hear, are balking at the pastor's efforts to get them to turn to each other and shake hands during the service. In our church the minister has upset a number of the older people, and a few of the younger, by trying to get us to sit closer together, and closer to the pulpit, in the usually empty forward pews. The resistance to this effort might surprise the founding fathers of the town, the original members of our church. According to one historical account, the seats in the rude first meetinghouse "were allotted strictly according to wealth, the front seats being reserved for the richest citizens. Indeed, until comparatively recently, when the universal custom of renting pews was abolished, the families of local prestige took the front pews, while the humbler worshippers slipped into the back and cheaper sittings, or occupied the seats for those who could pay nothing."

Although our two Protestant ministers have considerable support in their attempts to warm up our relationships to one another, to enhance the Christian togetherness of their congregations, they are up against a stubborn Yankee view that "no one can tell me where to sit" and "I will give my hand to whom I please." At today's Congregational discussion, some of the members said they felt more comfortable in the rear pews and would not come to church at all if they were roped off. The ropes will be removed.

• • •

The town is gearing up for the annual town meeting in October, but first we have a problem—something that cannot wait—so the selectmen have called a special town meeting for tonight. Three dozen townspeople turn up. Our purpose is simply to adopt the state's uniform building code. Like it or not, this and all other Connecticut towns must have building-code protection by October 1. By moving on the matter now—volunteering before being drafted, so to speak—we will be able to appoint a building inspector of our own choice rather than select an out-of-town man from a state-approved list. The main object, the First Selectman explains, is to "keep it local." In this cut-and-dried exercise, I agree to read off the motion from a prepared slip of paper. Seconded. Motion carried. Mission accomplished in twelve and a half minutes.

• • •

Time out to drive the dog to the vet. She had followed us as we rode the horses down past the sugar bush. She challenged a porcupine and came out of the woods with a face like a pincushion. A painless job of extraction was done.

• • •

The veterinarian is one of the busiest men in town. He is a tall, no-nonsense figure in long white coveralls who drives around the hills in his Oldsmobile looking after practically every animal in sight. He spends much of his long day vaccinating cows, inspecting livestock and giving tender care to an endless procession of ailing dogs, cats and other pets, but his fame in these parts and in equestrian circles elsewhere in the country rests on his skills as a horse doctor. Even though the tractor long ago replaced the workhorse on the farms hereabouts, the number of saddle horses for private pleasure riding has been rising dramatically. Besides, there is a breeding farm for champion Morgan horses just west of the village.

* * *

According to the National Geographic Society, there are some 5,000 full-time blacksmiths still operating in the United States, some earning from $20,000 to $30,000 a year. The blacksmith hired by local horse owners comes over from another town an hour's drive away. His infrequent visits touch off a scramble to make sure he gets to all the horses that need to be shod.

* * *

"People used to drive their horses to church and park in the church sheds. You weren't supposed to do business on Sunday, so one fellow would say, 'Well, John, if today was Monday, how much would you charge me if I bought your horse?' And the other would say, 'Well, if today was Monday, you could have my horse for 50 dollars.'"

* * *

"We were surrounded by farms when I first moved to the town. Now the small farmer in Connecticut has lost out almost entirely, in this region anyway. It's all gone to big farming where they have two to three thousand cows. The last fellow to go out of farming here had 80 cows, but that's not enough to support an expensive milk room and all the other costs. The only hope I feel is for the raising of beef. We've got some good pastureland for cattle."

* * *

"There's still some dairy farming, but that's phasing out fast. One farmer has just dropped out after breaking his leg. Sure, you still have people around here making a lot of milk, but it's funny the way some get bigger and some get littler. The number of working farms in Connecticut has been reduced tremendously, but they're still producing the same amount of milk. The Farm Bureau has trouble keeping up enough membership to have any kind of voice in Hartford. Used to be that the farmers and small-town folks ran things in this state. That's finished."

•   •   •

There's greater change in town when city folks buy a *farm* instead of a house on Main Street. . . . When a farm slips out of the hands of the real Yankees, a good many people wonder what is going to become of the town. . . . A town is more than so many human beings; it relies for its strength on people who live in certain ways, produce certain goods and values, and keep alive the old habits of life. The surest way to lose people who will do those things is to have them leave their farms.

CLARENCE M. WEBSTER, *Town Meeting Country*

•   •   •

"In some ways the town is less sociable now, looking at it from a farmer's point of view. The church and the Grange don't have the same hold on people, perhaps because there are so many other things to do. The Grange is still going strong, but you can't say it's a real farmers' organization anymore. You're lucky to find a farmer there, far as I can see."

•   •   •

"I've got a few hundred acres on what used to be a fruit farm. At one time there were quite a few orchards in town. Now it's a dairy farm with 125 cows. If I say so myself, it's an efficient farm. It has to be, otherwise I'd go out of business. Right now there are only seven dairy farms left in town, but a few families keep heifers.

"It used to be that you could get along producing four to six cans of milk a day and keep your family going, but now they talk about a *ton* of milk a day per man. Hand milking is finished, of course. You only use it when you're starting off a cow. We used to do our own bottling and sell the milk directly, but it became too expensive. Now we sell the milk to Borden's, and for all I know it's shipped back here in cartons.

"Years ago you did all the testing and figuring out on your own. It worked: people had milk. But today you're either efficient or you die. So we keep the most exact records on each cow, and I send out data which goes through an IBM machine in Cornell—costs me $40 a month—and I get back the recommended grain weights for each individual cow and so forth. All the emphasis these days is on better management and better breeding, which is mostly artificial breeding. The family bull is a thing of the past. Now you just telephone when you want the job done. The result of all this is that you have more milk but less farmers.

"You can no longer assume that the farmer's son will become a farmer. And it's hard to get labor. We have two hired hands who work from about five in the morning till five in the afternoon, with time off during the day. There's little work done in the evening. I get up myself at four in the morning. This early rising is from the days when the milk truck would come about seven and the milk had to cool off some. Now it comes at 8:30 but I still find it convenient to get up at four. I take catnaps during the day, if I'm not disturbed, and I fall asleep in the armchair while reading at nine or ten at night. When television first came along I used to watch quite a bit, but now I hardly ever look. I prefer a good book. As for the news, I get that on the radio as I go around on the tractor. Sunday mornings, I listen to the sermons."

· · ·

These crisp and brilliant but abbreviated autumn days remind us that winter is on its way. There are things to be done before the first snowflakes fly. We are finished with the garden. It just faded away, leaving us with tattered ranks of cornstalks. Only the other night we were out with a flashlight, checking on the last of the tomatoes and the threatening frost. It is time to take a chain saw into the woods and bring out wood for the winter.

The leaves have turned—and so melodramatically that the mountains all about seem to be on fire. The great sugar maple in front of the house has become a torch of flaming colors. Soon we will be driving up and down the mountain on a carpet of golden leaves. Even the native sons who have been watching the fall spectaculars for 60 or 70 years still catch their breath at the wonder of it all.

• • •

Several months have passed since the savings bank erected a big time-and-temperature sign in front of the bank building, just down the street from the crossroads. Some people, known as the "articulate few," have become quite agitated about the intrusion of a neon-lit advertising apparatus revolving 24 hours a day just across from the historic stone church and graveyard in the heart of the village. A "monstrosity" and an "eyesore," they insist in letters to the bank and the newspaper. An anti-sign petition has been introduced and the Historical Society has registered its disapproval. Fears have been voiced that this could be the beginning of a tawdry downtown of neon signs and drive-ins, since the business center does not come under the ordinance limiting the size of signs. Although meeting the protesters halfway by turning off the advertising portion of the apparatus at night, the out-of-town president of the bank insists that it is only doing the community a favor. "Some people," he writes, "have expressed a liking for the facility." Indeed, it appears that numerous townspeople are delighted to have an illuminated clock and thermometer close to Main Street and that most people wonder what the fuss is all about. For their part, say the editors of our local paper, "we would not dilute the force of our ecological efforts by extending the fight to public-service advertising signs. This is a capitalist economy and we like it that way."

• • •

"I think you're wrong about the bank sign—even if it is too big. I hate the neon sign in front of the package store, but I wouldn't say we have to get rid of it. I'd hate to have all the signs in town the same size. Even the shabby things are part of our way of life. I love this town because of its variety—all the things, good and bad, all the differences, the different kinds of people, the whole range of attitudes. You can be an individual here! I wouldn't want everything and everybody to be the same."

• • •

[There is a need] to respect the small unit, the neighborhood, in order to promote those qualities we associate, at least as an ideal, with the small town—meaning, I take it, a place where everyone has an identifiable face and is a recognizable and responsible citizen—not just a Social Security number, a draft card number, or a combination of digits on a computer. . . . I believe the greatest defect of the United States Constitution was its original failure, despite the example of the New England Township and the Town Meeting, to make this democratic local unit the basic cell of our whole system of government. For democracy, in any active sense, begins and ends in communities small enough for their members to meet face to face. Without such units, capable of independent and autonomous action, even the best-contrived central governments, state or federal, become party-oriented, indifferent to criticism, resentful of correction, and in the end, all too often, high-handed and dictatorial.

LEWIS MUMFORD, *The Urban Prospect*

• • •

The town still runs itself pretty much in the manner of the earliest settlement of two and a half centuries ago. Now, as then, we have face-to-face government. We air out our differences and make collective decisions in town meetings. The annual town meeting is held each October, and special sessions are called whenever necessary. Anyone with a big enough problem or grievance can get his fellow citizens together in a meeting—at least those who choose to attend—if he can collect 20 signatures on a petition. Even though only a small minority attends the average town meeting, we are governed by the town meeting. To get us through the day-to-day business of running the town, however, we elect a First Selectman and two other selectmen, as well as a Board of Finance, which keeps a beady eye on expenditures, and various other officials, boards and commissions.

• • •

The First Selectman, or mayor, is a full-time official who makes $8,500 a year, plus $1,000 expenses, and has an office in the town hall. The other selectmen put in less time and earn $600 each. The town clerk is the only other full-time official, making $6,500 for doing everything from issuing hunting licenses to keeping civic records shipshape. Most of the functionaries in our modest bureaucracy work part-time for a few hundred dollars a year, and we make heavy use of several dozen townspeople who labor without compensation on the boards and commissions.

It is not a faceless bureaucracy, beyond easy reach of the average man. The tax collector, visiting nurse, fire marshal, dog warden, tree warden, probate judge, assessors, registrars of voters, park and recreation commissioners, justices of the peace (who perform marriages and "quell riots"), members of the Board of Education and the others—they are all friends and neighbors. Like the teachers of our children, and the doctors and preachers and everyone else of importance, they are people we see on the street, meet in the stores, sit with in church.

The elected officials are more likely to be Republicans than Democrats, because like so many other rural communities, we have a long history of Republican majorities, but the Democrats are much in evidence. One of the three selectmen has to be a member of the minority party, and there is minority representation throughout the local government. The Board of Education is half Republican, half Democratic. Not that party labels matter much. Politics raises its head at election time, but it is ability and character that count over the long run.

• • •

"Even though the Republicans have outnumbered the Democrats here for as far back as anybody can remember, the Democrats have won once in a while. One fellow, Fred Johnson, ran for First Selectman, and he won by going over to the Hollow and telling all the Swedes over there that he'd save 'em money if they'd vote him in. He was an interesting First Selectman. He had a one-horse wagon and a wheelbarrow, and he took care of all the town roads and everything himself for a few dollars. He saved the town a lot of money. But someone said it was an awful job going around after him, putting things back where they were supposed to be."

●   ●   ●

"Let me tell you about the First Selectmen we've had in town since I've been here. You see, we had good old Ted for twenty-six years—a quarter of a century—and things poked along very nicely. People felt very comfortable with Ted, and he was very well liked. He built our paved road network. Did it very cleverly, at minimum expense. A lot of problems were deferred but they hadn't erupted in any urgent form. Equipment and buildings were pretty much run down, but taxes were kept low, and most local people were happy. And then when Art came in he was a real doer. He did many, many things in just a couple of years, so that the next two First Selectmen have been sort of living off the fat of what he did. He refurbished the equipment, painted the Community House and the town hall, installed lots of things in both places. All that cost money, and of course inflation had arrived, so he got tagged as a spender. Furthermore, he was a strong-minded fellow. There was only one way—his way. And so there was sort of a yearning for a breather from this hyperactive First Selectman.

"When Bill came in a few years ago I think he sensed this. He was our first Democratic First Selectman in a long, long time. The Republicans were split that year, and Bill was a very popular young man. So Bill ran the government as well as his garage in a nice relaxed way that sort of reminded you of Ted's regime. He would smoke his cigars and talk to everybody, get around the town a lot, so I'd say people were pretty well satisfied even if he might throw a lot of paper work into the wastebasket. Of course Art, as one of the other two Selectmen, was chafing at the bit. He'd make a lot of motions to get things done, and Walt would second them. This would put the burden on Bill to get them done. Well, he'd do some of them and postpone the rest. Bill would have had a lot of support if he had wanted to run for the job again, but he decided not to. And that brings us to Rusty, who gets a lot done in his own quiet way."

•   •   •

There was a certain inevitability about the election last year of our present First Selectman. His opponent, a likable, experienced attorney, not only had impressive credentials but said he would open up a local law office if elected. The town could use a law office. He even had a certain mystique as a man who grazes exotic animals on his Skiff Mountain pastures. But he had to campaign with three strikes against him. He was not a native son; he was a weekender who earned his living in New York. He had not held any previous office in town. And he was running on the Democratic ticket.

Rusty, on the other hand, was that amiable local fellow who drove a school bus. He had spent most of his life here even though it is not his birthplace. ("That's not his fault," someone generously observed.) He had gone to the local schools. He had long been connected with one of our oldest summer camps, and he had served on local boards and commissions. He was a fireman. All of this seemed to matter a lot more than his university degrees, his language skills or the city jobs he had once held in education and banking. At age 39 he was clearly capable, conscientious, energetic and experienced—and a Republican. But more important, he was well liked and well remembered.

"It was a dumfounding business, campaigning," he told me. "I was prepared to speak about issues, you know, but people would come up and tell me they remembered my red hair when I was a boy, or freckles, or some little thing. One fellow came up to me and said, 'You gave me a ride home fifteen years ago when I was drunk, and I've never forgotten it. You've got my vote! And as for that carpetbagger who's running on the other ticket . . . ,' and I thought, That's it! My poor opponent, he hasn't got a chance."

• • •

The other day I asked the First Selectman to stop by at the house and tell me what it was like being a First Selectman. Some things he mentioned:

— "Well, it's the best job I've ever had. I was working in the international division of a bank in New York and I enjoyed it very much, but this is different. I can use my head, but I don't have to sit at a desk all day. I'm outside a lot, keeping fit and active, moving around town. Of course I spend a lot of time and lots of nights at meetings, but nobody's riding herd on me over the hours. If I have some family business, I can just take off."

— "The job has a lot of variety. People call me with their complaints, and I get a lot of requests for information. The other day I got a phone call from a hospital in some far-off town to tell me that a man there had just died of TB and since he had no family and his last address of record was this town, we would have to bury him. 'Thank you very much, Doctor,' I said, and started scurrying around for an undertaker. My wife and I were mourners at the burial."

— "An awful lot of things come back to the First Selectman. In the absence of a specific board, commission or department, he becomes that board, commission or department. Because we have no police department, I'm the police chief. Which means I sign all the pistol permits and a few reports. I'm also the welfare department. The dogcatcher resigned a couple of weeks ago, so I automatically became the dogcatcher until I found a new one."

— "A First Selectman has some fantastic powers, but at the same time he is absolutely limited by what the town meeting tells

him he can do. I suppose in other parts of the country people
think the New England town meeting is an anachronism, not in
tune with modern problems. Certainly if a town gets too big, one
of two things happens. Either you've got a government of the
very, very few, the ones who take the time to be involved, which
is unrepresentative, or you get tremendous turnouts and end up
with unwieldy meetings. I don't know exactly when this cutoff
point comes, but I think what we have here is satisfactory. Unfortunately, the town meetings aren't as colorful as they used to
be. In fact, they're pretty dull. We used to have some real characters, and it was their night to howl."

— "One of the difficulties of small-town government is that it's
hard to find people with experience, though of course not all the
jobs are too demanding. People go into local politics for different
reasons. For some, it's an outright desire to be involved in the
political welfare of the town. In others, a desire to learn something or gain some practical experience. Someone in real estate
might want to become an assessor to add to his background about
appraisal and property values. In my own case, I had come back
to the town in the spring of '66 after working for the bank. I was
doing my camp work full time and driving the school bus to tide
me over in the wintertime. I decided I wanted to stay here. I was
a registered Republican and sort of interested in things. So, a few
months before the 1967 election, I let the Republican chairman
know I was interested. He asked me what I would like. I said the
Board of Finance since I could bring some experience to the job.
He said they were all set in that department and suggested the
Board of Tax Review. I protested that I didn't know anything
about it. 'Well, don't worry,' he said, 'Frank's on it now, and he
doesn't know anything about it either.' Well, that's how I
started. The town clerk sort of carried me through the first
year."

— "You get to wear a lot of hats in a small town. We have a
lot of versatile people here who do more things than they ever
would if they lived in the city. Besides having this job I'm treas-

urer of the Nursing Association, and I'm in the fire department and involved in other things. I'm out with the road crew a lot because I'm interested in that end of the business."

—"The First Selectman used to be the road boss because he was only paid $1,200, and he could make some more money by working on the road crew and paying himself the hourly rate. The two jobs went together. This was typical small-town stuff, but it was a practical block to competent people, like retired businessmen, who could run a good office but who could not or would not go out and drive a dump truck. We separated the jobs during Art's time when it was decided to pay the First Selectman a living wage and pay someone else to be the road foreman."

— "When I first got in I involved myself a lot with the road work just to see what was going on. After all, the First Selectman is empowered to enter into agreements with the highway commissioner concerning the town-aid road funds. Except for education, most of our money goes into keeping up the roads; the rest is peanuts. I wanted to be able to drive all the equipment. My duty during a snowstorm is theoretically nothing, but practically I get involved setting the wheels in motion. With some of these storms that start in the late afternoon, just to divvy up the work and cut the overtime a little, I would take charge of the evening part and send the men home around midnight. Then the foreman would get up about four in the morning and call out the crew again, if he had to, to work before school bus time."

— "The selectmen's budget takes a lot of work. In a small town the selectmen seem to get involved in financial planning for the other people who are spending money. I'm the one who's in touch with the bankers on the school and sewer borrowing. You might expect the Board of Finance to be doing all that, but it's almost traditional in a small town for the selectmen to handle it and report to the Board of Finance. It's a practical matter. The banker would prefer to deal with one selectman who's working with the problem from day to day than try to get a bunch of part-time people to agree to something."

— "Unfortunately the new state regulations and other things are making all the local government offices so complicated that they're getting beyond the part-time good citizen. We may have to have professional people in the future, but where are they going to come from and how are we going to pay them? I suppose regionalization of towns is the answer, but you lose a lot when you go that route."

— "I think regionalization makes sense for the careful development of an area like the upper river valley, but I don't like us to be pushed too quickly into regionalizing everything—every assessor's office and so on. I like to feel I'm not two-faced about this, because I'm not an enemy of the state. I go to them for most of the complicated problems. I just resent the state encroaching on us for the things we do well or do better. When we have a one-shot emergency welfare problem we're much better than the state Welfare Department because we can do it quickly without a caseworker or filling out a lot of forms. But of course we don't have the machinery to deal with a continuing problem. On tax collecting, our overhead is about two cents on the dollar. I don't think the state Tax Department can make that claim. The state gives us a lot of money for education, and that's good, but they set standards that soak it up. They give us a 50 percent reimbursement on school buildings, but to qualify for that you have to build them their way, and I think—in fact, I know very well— that you could build an excellent modern building, well-heated, -lighted, -ventilated, for a lot less than we're made to, maybe 50 percent less."

— "One thing I hated seeing while I was on the Tax Review Board was the way the farms disappeared one by one. But of course this has happened without the physical appearance of the town changing very much. Yet. The question mark is which way these big properties are going to go now. Enough individuals to hold them together or big developments? We might be in for really unsettling growth one day."

— "Right now I think this is an ideal place to live in. If you look at some of the other towns near us, some have become too citified, some are too scattered, some have too great a spread between rich and poor. They probably disparage us for being off on a tangent and less distinguished in some ways, but I think we're better balanced. There's a lack of phoniness here. It's been a political asset to me. I can ride my bike or drive my car or arrive on foot at some function, and it doesn't make any difference. I can get out my tux now and then, or I can appear in my jump suit, depending on the occasion, and people take me for what I am and what I do. It's a good life. We're living up by the lake now, and I hope to farm it a bit. I like people, but I like the open spaces too. It's great when you can have both."

•   •   •

Every so often the valley fills up with a fog and the village becomes a damply beautiful ghost town. Driving down the mountain is like a slow-motion dive into a pool of white mist. But more often it is the other way around. Driving up the mountain road from the clear village, we head into a foamy surf of fog rolling downhill. Groping our way for the last mile or so, headlights serving as antennae, we finally make out the barnyard lights.

•   •   •

Time for the annual town meeting: the 231st in the history of this settlement, which was running its own affairs half a century before the adoption of the United States Constitution. This is a historic occasion that ought to be the biggest day of the year. It is face-to-face democracy in its purest form. But, sad to say, only 54 attend out of an electorate of more than a thousand. There is no excitement, little discussion. All cut-and-dried, and all over in 41 minutes.

•   •   •

"The town meetings aren't as lively as they used to be. Instead of the school gymnasium we would meet in Bulls Hall, where the post office is now, and folks would be packed in pretty tight. I used to get a kick out of the Templeton brothers, who were two different breeds of cat. They were just the opposite. Whatever Will was in favor of, Dave would be against. They fought like anything. One night they argued back and forth, bucking each other, and by and by Dave got up and said to the people at large, 'Ladies and gentlemen, as you know, I differ from my brother very much. I don't mind telling you right now that he's a damned liar!' Well, you could have heard a pin drop."

• • •

"There was an artist who lived here who opposed the library and opposed the Community House and in fact resisted anything he didn't start. He was a clever talker, and he got in with a crowd of hicks who were against anything new. There would be terrible battles with people who were trying to get things done. We had to have the police in one time to control the meeting."

• • •

Local control has clearly been stabbed in the back in the legislative halls of Hartford.

EDITORIAL

• • •

"The reason the town meeting isn't what it used to be is that we're dancing to Hartford's tune. Basically, what happens is that the state says you've got to do it, like putting in the sewer system, whether you like it or not. No longer do you make the decision whether to do it or don't do it, which is the exciting part: you feel you have the power. But now it's just a question of who's going to pay for it."

• • •

"I remember the first town meeting I attended here, not so many years ago. There was a discussion about the school kids up

on Skiff Mountain having to wait in the rain for the bus. Not
having any shelter in bad weather. Someone asked why the problem has come up now after all these years. He was told that the
kids used to stand in an empty mausoleum in the cemetery when
it rained and then come running out when the bus came along.
But then some man died and they filled up the mausoleum, leaving the children to stand on the road getting wet. I remember
the discussion, but I don't think the town ever did put up a shelter."

                         •   •   •

Town Meeting: Flavor Gone, but Spirit Lingers
                            HEADLINE, *The New York Times*

                         •   •   •

It is as old as the *Mayflower*. It has been acclaimed as "the
quintessence of democracy" and put down as "horse-and-buggy
government in the jet age." It isn't what it used to be, but then
nothing is. Despite everything, it is still going strong in New
England.

Way, way back, the annual town meeting would bring out of
the woods and pull out of the woodwork folks who had not been
seen in the village all year. They would come for the day, bringing their lunch with them or buying baked beans and corn bread
from the church ladies. The meeting would go on for hours
in the smoky town hall or in whatever space was deemed large
enough to hold all the farmers and villagers. There would be
much speechmaking and moments of high emotion, wild accu-
sations, words of wisdom and outbursts of temper. Old rivals
might even come to blows.

Money would often be at the heart of the matter. "The curse
of the average Town Meeting in New England villages is ig-
norance," said an area newspaper in 1885. "Either to make a saving of a few hundred dollars now, a proposed temporary additional expense is voted down, although it would save many

hundreds of dollars in the future, or else the unwary voters allow some beguiling but impractical scheme, full of expense, to be lightly lowered on them while they comfortably dream that they are to be benefitted, not knowing that they will finally wake up and cry out unavailingly when they feel the pressure of a great weight."

The first town meetings in Colonial times were intended to make "orders necessary for the good government of the community." Later on, the principal business of the town meeting was the election of officers who would govern from one annual session to the next. More recently in Connecticut, elections of officers have been held separate from the town meeting, and they are assigned clear-cut administrative duties. The town meeting functions as a minilegislature. Every voter, if he takes the trouble to attend, is his own lawmaker. It is pure people power, but it depends on a modest size. If a town gets too big, things get out of hand. A number of grown-up small towns have adopted the representative town meeting. In Westport, for example, the 38 unpaid members of the non-partisan representative town meeting are elected for two-year terms and conduct their business in public. The townspeople who attend their sessions are invited to speak up, but they cannot vote. The state's largest "towns," of course, including Hartford and New Haven, have long since become too big for any form of town meeting. They have their mayors and councils and so many civic employees that the personal touch, the quick response of neighborly government, is a thing of memory. This is the face of the future, or so the figures on rising population suggest. For now, however, in four fifths of the towns, the town meeting cantankerously survives.

●   ●   ●

E. B. White observed some years ago that "New Englanders are jealous of their right to govern themselves as they like, but in my town we have learned that town meeting is no place to decide anything. We thrash out our problems well in advance, working in small queues and with a long history of spite as a background. The meeting is just to make everything legal."

Here, too, the meeting—broadly speaking—is just to make everything legal, although anyone is free to stand up and speak his piece. For some time now our affairs have been in good hands, things gone along smoothly, and we have argued out the big problems in special meetings and hearings and around the town, so we see no point in dragging out the annual gathering just for the fun of it. The idea is to get on with the business and go home.

Which is the way things went at this year's town meeting. It was called for eight o'clock of a brisk October day. A number of villagers strolled over to the Center School, but most of us arrived by car. We chatted with one another on the way into the gymnasium. This spacious, brightly lit hall is functional enough, but it lacks the atmosphere of the town meeting setting of years past—the wood chunks snapping in the glowing cast-iron stove, the smell of leather and wet wool, the uneven floor damp with tracked-in outdoors. Sitting on metal folding chairs, we faced the town clerk and the three selectmen, who were seated behind tables underneath a raised-up basketball net. A few members of the press had placed themselves at another table to the side.

We began with the election of a moderator. The town clerk read the warning. There was a motion and a seconding of the motion on the first item: "to receive and act upon the reports of Town Boards." This was quickly approved without discussion. The same for item number two: authorizing the selectmen and treasurer to do the necessary borrowing. And so it went, down the list: authorizing the selectmen to take up town road matters with the state highway commissioner; appointments to the Park and Recreation Commission; something about building-inspection fees; disposal of state aid to the town's nursing services; and so on. We had little or nothing to say as we approved a complicated sewer ordinance, but we indulged ourselves in a brisk debate about an ordinance regulating outdoor fires. This could have been the stuff on flaming controversy, this latest interference in our private lives. Outdoor fires were to be confined to "an approved type of incinerator" except when permission was given by the fire marshal or one of his deputies. We would have to think twice about putting a match to our autumn leaves and grocery cartons. But we listened to the explanations—the fire hazard during dry periods, the way the volunteer firemen were being run ragged by campfires and bonfires that had gotten out of hand—and gave our assent. Meeting adjourned.

•   •   •

One of our Skiff Mountain neighbors had to get up early this morning while it was still dark. Driving away from his house, going by a hayfield, he saw a couple of deerjackers taking aim at a large deer standing transfixed in their headlights. He stopped his car, opened the door and then slammed it shut. The noise startled the deer and it bounded off before the hunters could shoot. He drove on, his good deed for the day done.

•   •   •

Excitement at the high school. Someone telephoned the principal this morning at 11:25 to advise him, anonymously, to look for an important message in the vice principal's mailbox. The unsigned note warned that a bomb would go off somewhere in the school at 12 noon. The school was evacuated in a minute and a half, thanks partly to the concentration of many pupils in the cafeteria. After some milling about on the lawn the pupils were sent home while officials, police and a bomb squad rushed over from Hartford searched for a bomb that wasn't there. No one thought that "it can't happen here." We remember that it did happen, just a year and a month ago, when those four kids on drugs bombed the school in the predawn hours.

•   •   •

Although the town has its share of suicides, accomplished and attempted, we seem to be getting more than our share of people who drive in here to do away with themselves. Just a month ago a man from Bridgeport killed himself with a shotgun on Schaghticoke road. Today the body of another Bridgeport man, another suicide, was discovered in a state park.

• • •

These are busy days. The politicians are in full cry. Election coming up. Someone has installed a large trailer in full view on the highway, just above the village, so now there is a movement underway to ban trailers. Columbus Day filled up the town with parents visiting the boarding schools, and city people driving about our twisty roads looking over the fall foliage. The whole township was transformed into an artist's palette. The Congregational church's Harvest Fair and Auction—men working the old-time cider press, the ladies cooking doughnuts—made about $2,000. The Boy Scouts have been collecting bundles of scrap paper. The library and PTA joined forces for a Book and Bake Sale. Tonight is Halloween, and there are lighted pumpkins with carved-out faces set out in front of many homes. Kids wearing masks and bedsheets are knocking on front doors, asking, "Trick or treat?" The teen-agers of the Pilgrim Fellowship and the Catholic Youth Organization are not only going about with orange-and-black boxes, raising money for the United Nations Children's Fund, but they have organized a children's costume party at the parish house.

• • •

The resident trooper has put out a warning. We should be on the lookout for thieves who have been going through a number of towns stealing grandfather's clocks. According to the magazine *Yankee* we should also keep a weather eye cocked for robbers who have been removing antique weathervanes from barns all over New England.

• • •

She rested at home. She listened to the village noises common to all the world, jungle or prairie; sounds simple and charged with magic—

dogs barking, chickens making a gurgling sound of content, children at play, a man beating a rug, wind in the cottonwood trees, a locust fiddling, a footstep on the walk, jaunty voices of Bea and a grocer's boy in the kitchen, a clinking anvil, a piano—not too near.

Twice a week, at least, she drove into the country with Kennicott, to hunt ducks in lakes enameled with sunset, or to call on patients who looked up to her as the squire's lady and thanked her for toys and magazines. Evenings she went with her husband to the motion pictures and was boisterously greeted by every other couple; or, till it became too cold, they sat on the porch, bawling to passers-by in motors, or to neighbors who were raking the leaves. The dust became golden in the low sun; the street was filled with the fragrance of burning leaves.

SINCLAIR LEWIS, *Main Street*

•   •   •

Winter coming fast. Plumes of smoke from burning leaves are rising in the hills. The last apples thud to the ground. The horses are shaggy in their new coats. The children start wearing scarves and mittens as they set out for school. The night winds are biting cold, and the frost is on the pumpkin. We had our first flurries of snow as early as October 17—just enough to lay a thin sheet on our mountaintops. Now the flurries thicken, and the whole town is dusted white. One old townsman, who knows his seasons, predicts an early, long and rigorous winter.

•   •   •

If this should ever become a big town, the historian might say that this was the year it began. For some months now, a $3-million apartment project—a condominium—has been under construction at the top of Main Street, just within the unzoned fire district in the heart of the township. The first apartments have just been completed. They were opened for inspection this morning. Purchase price for the owner-occupier: about $35,000. Ultimately, there will be some 85 "garden units" and "town house units" stretching from the new white picket fence by the highway toward the rocky slopes of the eastern hills. Happily, the barnlike two-story structures of pitched roofs and white clapboards have a traditional New England look, fitting in well with the over-all appearance of the village. There seems to be general agreement that this is an economic shot in the arm, certainly a big help to taxpayers, without being too big a development for the town to be able to swallow comfortably. And yet there is a whiff of regret in the air, a sense of the future closing in.

• • •

"Every time you want to do something in this town there's some damned ordinance that says you can't."

• • •

The Planning and Zoning Commission has come up with a new zoning regulation that bans mobile homes or trailers from being used as residences in the town. It had been popularly assumed that the existing town ordinance requiring 30,000 square feet of land for a trailer, as against 40,000 for a house, would be discouragement enough. The appearance of the mobile home on the highway has changed the picture. The widespread apprehension that the townscape might become "littered with metal monsters," as one man put it, has spurred the commissioners into quick action. Not that everyone is in favor of the ban. It was heatedly debated tonight at a hearing in the school gym. Some people said they were not offended by the appearance of trailers. One man, who owns about 200 acres, said he might put a trailer on his property no matter what: "You'd have a helluva time finding it." Several senior citizens described the merits of trailer living. The morality of a ban was argued. Wasn't the town discriminating against poorer people who could not afford to buy a house but could manage a trailer? But mention was made of the experiences of other towns with trailers and trailer camps. They were ugly. They caused trouble and pollution. This appeared to be the consensus. No trailers.

• • •

"What zoning has done is to keep us from being swamped. We could have become a bedroom town with these miserable cheap subdivisions all over. I know we've made it more difficult for poor people with large families to move here, but as it is we've had a tremendous increase in the number of children and school enrollment. We're just trying not to be overwhelmed."

•   •   •

"The zoning fight in this town went on for decades. I mean that. It started way back before World War II, in the 1930s, and, as I recall, it was defeated four times. The first time it was voted in, there was such a howl that they threw it right out. We finally got it through for good a few years later. This was a very intelligent town, but we also had a bunch of hicks—though I suppose I shouldn't call them that—who'd come down from the mountain whenever we tried to put anything good over. It was the backcountry versus the intellectual side: those who hated any kind of change and those who wanted culture. A lot of the people against zoning were farmers who were afraid that it would take away their rights. Now they see that their rights have been stabilized by zoning. The trouble in the beginning was that we hired experts, who would tell us that something had to be so many exact feet from a curb, as if they were zoning for a city. Well, we soon found out that this town hates experts. So then we decided to draw up the zoning regulations ourselves. In meeting after meeting all factions came in—farmers, businessmen, the intellectuals—and they told what they wanted. Eventually we got a zoning law that worked. Coming on top of the ordinances that the Garden Club and the women had put over, it has proved to be pretty effective. We've saved ourselves from the junky look of some towns."

•   •   •

"We used to have some real knockdown, drag-out political battles in this town, but now—well, it's all very gentlemanly. There's not much excitement left. No one you can really feel angry about. There's not much difference between the parties or the candidates, far as I can see."

• • •

We have had a calm election season. It is an off year, pretty much, for local politics. We elected the selectmen and the other town officials last year. This time we have a couple of posts to fill as well as the election of a congressman, senator and the governor. Since the town is about two thirds Republican we are seldom surprised by the outcome on the local offices. The suspense is generated by the regional and statewide campaigns. We are one of the smallest towns in a 47-town congressional district of half a million, but the candidates turn up every so often to shake a few hands and stroll along Main Street. As election day approaches, the Republicans put on their customary beer party in the Community House, and the Democrats get on the telephone to urge the faithful to get out and vote.

• • •

Until 1967 the little towns of Connecticut had a powerful voice in state affairs. Many sparsely populated country settlements of a few hundred or a few thousand inhabitants had two seats in the lower house of the legislature, the same as cities of more than 100,000 people. (Our town lost one of its original two seats long ago when a portion to the east was split off to form a new town.) The result was that one tenth of all voters elected more than half the members. The rural Republicans thought this was only right; everyone knew how much wiser a down-to-earth countryman is than a city fellow. The urban Democrats objected. The courts finally compelled reform. Today, our town has one sixth of a representative (and one thirteenth of a senator) in Hartford.

• • •

Up here in the hill country, this area of small but venerable farms, we are catching our breath after tending to such fundamental matters as getting the hay into the mow, filling the silos and stowing the garden's yield in the freezer and the root cellar. The country fair is over. The political campaign has run its course. Tomorrow we shall go to the polls and, with luck, the dust will settle and the uproar die down before the first snow flies.

HAL BORLAND, *Countryman: A Summary of Belief*

• • •

The girls have come home from a hawk watch. A party of bird lovers journeyed this morning to a well-known observation point to have a look at the migrating birds. The count by day's end was more than a hundred sharp-shinned hawks, 25 red-tails, nine sparrow hawks, three ospreys, two marsh hawks, two red-shouldered hawks and one bald eagle.

• • •

Election day. A clean sweep for the Republicans. Their candidates beat the Democrats by about 590 votes to 270. Eighty-one percent of the eligible voters turned out.

• • •

Now, in November, the town has closed into itself. It is settling down for the winter. The summer people departed many weeks ago, not to be seen again until spring, and the last of the tourists disappeared when the autumn leaves blew off the trees. The landscape has opened up, and the horizon has been pushed back, now that the foliage is gone. Everything in view seems more sharply defined, as if we are seeing an etching after many months of watercolors. Crawford's is advertising turkeys, McIntosh apples and "a keg of lean salt pork, still in the brine." The American Legion post has been sponsoring early-afternoon turkey shoots on consecutive Sundays. The three churches are planning an ecumenical Thanksgiving service, the money from the offering to go to a drug rehabilitation center in a nearby town. The annual bazaar at St. Andrew's is coming up soon. There are crisp, bright, good-to-be-alive days, a time for family reunions and the re-

newed pleasures of log fires. We take Thanksgiving Day seriously, knowing that we have much to be thankful for.

•   •   •

Three desperadoes have just held up a bank in a neighboring
town. They came careening through our village, trying to make a
getaway. Trooper Andy chased them down the highway, through
the covered bridge and around back roads as they headed west.
At times both cars were going over 100 miles per hour. A second
trooper joined in the chase. Bullets were exchanged. Then dozens of police and even a helicopter took over. Finally the bandits
surrendered when they found the highway blocked by a sand-
filled tractor-trailer that the police had commandeered and
stretched across the road.

This was the biggest crime story around here since the day a
year and a half ago when the charred and decomposed bodies of
two strangers were discovered in the woods by the river road.
The case had all the earmarks of a gangland execution. The unknown victims had apparently been shot and set afire several
months earlier. No one knows why our town was selected for
this purpose, but we have had to go to the trouble and expense
of burying the bodies in metal coffins in a shallow grave in the
Congregational cemetery—just in case they need to be examined
again for identification.

•   •   •

"We have some burglary, and we get blamed for it statistically
because it's reported where it occurs, but a lot of it is done by
foreigners—outsiders—who cruise in here and hit these empty
camps and summer places. For the most part it's not local people
who are doing it. When friends visit us from out of town they are
absolutely dumfounded that I leave the keys in the car and leave
the house unlocked. But I have two sets of manners: one for here
and another for New York. When I go down there the first thing
I do is push the lock buttons on the car."

•   •   •

"There's not much crime here in absolute numbers, but because the statistical base is so small, we have a rather high *rate* in some categories, and some years it shoots way up. Many years ago, down in the Hollow, we had a rather unsavory case of a baby found dead in a milk can. Prior to that we didn't have a known infanticide rate, and that one versus 1,800 people gave us a fantastically high rate for that year. We were right up there with the best of them."

•   •   •

"Here is our view on law enforcement: We want our trooper to be real tough on outsiders. Crack down on the speeders and anyone else who breaks the law. But somehow we think we can be the exception. If he catches us doing something wrong, then we holler."

•   •   •

The resident state trooper's latest statistical report of police activities conducted in the town over a one-year period reveals 118 criminal investigations, 62 motor vehicle investigations and 250 calls for miscellaneous police service which did not warrant formal investigation.

Just going by the numbers, and putting aside the various auto accidents and improper use of motor vehicles, it would seem that the most common misdeeds—done by us or to us—are larceny, breaking and entering, breaches of the peace, shoplifting and intoxication. Violent crime is virtually nonexistent. An occasional car is stolen, some private property is damaged, people are stopped for throwing trash on the highway. The statistics show one forgery, one suspicious fire, one harassing phone call, one case of trespassing and one missing person. In the previous reporting year there were four cases of "sex (miscellaneous)," but there is none this time.

•   •   •

People usually think the woods in a new country must be all full of wild animals. I suppose they are, more or less, but some of the wild

animals thrive much better where the land has been cultivated and
then grown up again. In Gramp's time there was practically no deer
in southern Vermont. The first one was brought in by the state from
over in New York and released with tags in their ears. I never knew of
any deer until I got to be fourteen or fifteen years old. . . . Now
they're a regular pest in Windham County.

WALTER NEEDHAM, *A Book of Country Things*

• • •

It is best to drive slowly on these back roads at night. A deer
will suddenly appear in the headlights—or a raccoon, a porcupine
or a skunk. Sometimes a pheasant or a wandering cat. Now and
then a fox. Last night, driving home from a meeting, I was going
slowly enough, keeping an eye out for furry creatures on the
road, when a deer came flying out of the woods and crashed
into my right front fender. It was instant death for the deer and
$300 worth of damage to the car.

• • •

NEW ENGLAND VILLAGE, 1942

Here are the hills, the river and the school,
  The Grange, the stores, three churches. Down a way
You'll find the drowsing station, where the rule
  Is two trains up, and two trains down, each day.

St. Andrew's churchyard rests an ancient guild
  Of Howlands, Wathleys, Winegars and Lains
Who, by their way of living, helped to build
  The mood of peace the village still retains.

Yet look again, lest you conclude the world
  Spins past these homes. No leafy street but one
Bright window has a little flag unfurled
  With every star of blue an absent son.

Loving its own, but loving freedom more
  This tiny village, too, has gone to war.

• • •

Milton Bracker's description of our town in the aftermath of Pearl Harbor was published in *The New York Times* on August 11, 1942. Today, more than a quarter century later, we are again at war. Though undeclared, it has become the longest war in the country's history. Young men from these simple New England communities have been sent to fight from village to village, or to drop bombs on hill and hamlet, in small nations of Indochina which pose no threat to us and which few of us could easily find on the map. As in other towns across the nation, they go off to war and return from war without fanfare. There are no little flags in the windows, no stars of blue. There are no brass bands, no patriotic orations or parades down Main Street, no talk of the heroes of Vietnam. Every so often there is a faint little stir when a local boy returns from the other side of the world and slips quietly back into the life of the town. This week a favored son has returned home: a handsome youth, remembered as a fine student and athlete. A Ranger staff sergeant who had volunteered for service, he was wounded in combat and died during a helicopter rescue operation. Townspeople of all faiths have gathered in the Congregational church for a moving memorial service, and we have buried him with full military honors in the old green graveyard. He was 21.

•   •   •

Our local snowmobile enthusiasts have organized themselves into a club called the Schaghticoke Slyders. They have laid plans, through the chamber of commerce, to hold a snowmobile rally in January. Out-of-towners from all over the state will be invited to take part. The local paper says that if all goes well, the town could become "the snowmobile capital of Connecticut." Others are less enthusiastic. In fact, quite a few take a dim view of snowmobilers as noisemakers, trespassers, enemies of wildlife, destroyers of wintertime solitude, and "a downright menace," comparable to speedboat maniacs on a lake of quiet sailboats. If this is to become their Mecca, will we meet the same unhappy fate as the little tucked-away village of Lime Rock, which was transformed a few years ago into one of the foremost auto-racing centers in the East?

I ask the postmaster about it. His family has been in the town for over 200 years. "As long as I've lived here," he assures me, "people have always been worrying about one thing or another —worrying about what's going to happen to the town. But most of those things just never happen. It turned out that they had nothing to worry about in the first place."

• • •

In what may be an inspiration to other folks in this hirsute era, a local mother dropped in at the barber shop and asked about Gift Certificates. Nick never went in for them, but a deal was made. The mother is giving her son a card entitling him to five haircuts in the coming year. If he wants to get one of them now, so much the better. It's to be a surprise, so we cannot print the name.

                                                            The Good Times Dispatch

• • •

The year is running out. The days are short now; the darkness closes in by late afternoon. The hunters have been active for some weeks, going after deer and ducks, and ice fishermen can be seen on the lakes and ponds, but the snow is deepening, and we have had some days of bone-chilling cold. People stay indoors mostly and bundle up well when they venture outside. Sinclair Lewis, speaking of Gopher Prairie digging in for the winter, said that in the northern states of the Middle West, winter is not a season but an industry. Here in lower New England, we have it easier, and our modern oil furnaces and electrical appliances greatly lift the weight of the long cold, but we do have to pay attention. Winter in these hills can be rigorous and the snow-storms savage. Last year's heaviest snowfall came just at Christmastime; it was hard going just getting to the barn to feed the horses.

The woodshed is full. The storm windows are up. There are studded snow tires on all four wheels of our front-wheel-drive

Saab. A truckload of chips and sawdust has been brought in and poured into the silo so that the horses will have bedding in their stalls. The loose windows on the barn have been battened down and the snow blower bolted on the tractor. Down in the village, behind the town hall, the big yellow snowplows have been mounted on the trucks, and a full supply of sand is ready. Red marker sticks have been fixed to the Main Street fire hydrants so that they can be found in the snow.

The river began to ice up during the first week of December, but it thawed after a succession of warm nights. Then the temperature dropped below freezing and stayed there. A northeaster blew in. Now the river is frozen solid until March. We are guaranteed a white Christmas.

WINTER

WINTER LIGHT. Frosty windows. Icicles on the eaves. A stillness in the forest. Cars with skis on the roof heading north. Shirts on the clothesline stiff as boards. Everywhere, except for the steaming manure pile behind the barn, a heavy shroud of snow. The silver birches are almost luminous in the dark woods. There are animal tracks stitching the snow-quilted hayfields. The shaggy horses stand with their hindquarters to the cold wind. Except for the red cardinal who visits our backyard and the orange caress of the setting sun, we live in a black-and-white world. Or, better said, a world with variations of grayness. But we are rescued from dreariness by the joy and sparkle of the Christmas season.

It begins here a little later than in the city; our stores are too few and modest to impose a commercial Christmas of any consequence. In their own good time the shopkeepers put up the appropriate decorations and place gift advertisements in the newspaper. Strings of colored lights are plugged in on Main Street, and the Garden Club members bring out the wreaths and floral pieces they have made for our public buildings. Several citizens, to earn a little Christmas money, announce that cut-your-own trees are available on their land.

As Christmas Day approaches, we move closer to the true spirit of the season. Young people come home from college, and seldom-seen relatives drive up for family get-togethers. We find ourselves at candlelit dinner tables and in living rooms glowing with the light of burning logs. There are Christmas programs at the schools, nativity pageants and special services at the churches, a pancakes-and-sausages breakfast at the parish house, and parties for the town youngsters, complete with Santa Claus. The boys and girls of the Scouts and the church youth groups go about singing carols in the village, joined by passersby, and in the retirement homes for the old folks.

Now, on Christmas Eve, just before midnight, when the children are snug in bed and their tired parents wrap the last of the presents, the ice-bright stars shine benevolently on this quiet little town. The snow falls softly.

•   •   •

Overheard at a publisher's cocktail party, from the lips of a visiting British author: "I must say, I've enjoyed your country. Spent the weekend in Connecticut. First time I've been to the interior."

The New Yorker

•   •   •

Talk about the Perils of Pauline! We learn that there has been another stay of execution; passenger service on our arthritic railroad will not be discontinued. Not quite yet. The Interstate Commerce Commission has been holding hearings, receiving petitions, reading our letters, hearing from our congressmen. The First Selectman has been in the thick of the struggle to save the trains. "We're not wiped out yet," he says.

•   •   •

The town clerk reports that all the justices of the peace elected back in November have been duly sworn, but there was a little mix-up along the way. One of our veteran JPs had run for office again and was elected—or so he thought. In fact, his party, the Democrats, had mistakenly filed the name of his son, Earl, Jr., an independent, with the secretary of state before the election, and it was junior, not senior, who was elected and who now holds the office. No problem: the father has graciously given way to the son.

* * *

Two official reminders. The post office is asking rural route patrons to be sure to shovel out the approach to their mailboxes. If the boxes are snowbound, the carrier is not obliged to deliver the mail. And the resident trooper, noting that Christmas wrappings and boxes have been strewn in places along the highway, says that "failure to secure a load" on the way to the dump is a motor vehicle offense.

* * *

"I was at the dump one day, just poking around, and I came across this old schoolboy's album from the nineteenth century. I found my father's name in it."

* * *

The town dump is one of our most important institutions. Officially, it is a "sanitary landfill," the place where people personally deposit their trash if they do not hire a local boy or a private contractor to haul it away. Like many other small communities across the country, we have no town garbage or trash collection service. The dump is a do-it-yourself operation. A writer for the *Irish Times* of Dublin, describing the American way of life as seen in East Hampton, Long Island, said that "one can almost gauge the social climbing aspirations of much of the working and middle classes in this community on the basis of whether or not they haul their own refuse to the dump. Some people would die rather than be seen carting and unloading their own garbage. Others, of course, don't care for such social distinctions one way or the other."

It is perhaps a measure of our happy condition as a democratic and unpretentious small town that our dump, on the Sundays and Mondays when it is open for business, is a meeting place for local people of various incomes and interests. Like the parking lot of the school after a town meeting or a budget hearing, it is a convenient setting for the exchange of gossip and information. One can also find an odd piece of furniture or an old radio in the midst of the cans, bottles, bricks, tires, scrap lumber and worn-out television sets. Every now and then there is an exchange of sheepish grins as the man who has thrown away an old pump picks up the stepladder just thrown away by the man reaching for the pump.

*   *   *

The town had no public dump until 1934 and no serious disposal problem until recent years. People used to feed scraps to the pigs and chickens, build up compost heaps with waste food, get rid of paper in the wood stove or fireplace and put up their own preserves instead of depending on canned and frozen foods. They did not come home from the grocery with every last item elaborately packaged. Today, as we come close to drowning ourselves in junk mail, plastic containers and no-return bottles, all these towns are plagued with disposal problems. As each dump site fills up they search for another location or else turn their minds to expensive technological solutions. If regionalization ever takes hold in this area, it will probably be because the towns have decided that they must either dispose together or singly waste away.

*   *   *

Winter doesn't get any worse. It just seems that way. Our stock of snow shrank by a full 12 inches in the rain and thaw early this January week. But this still is a land of plenty, so far as snow is concerned. For those who like it, we sullenly rejoice.

EDITORIAL

*   *   *

I ask one of the selectmen a question. We have, right at hand for everyone, free of charge, the great outdoors and its multiple blessings—a white-water river, streams, lakes, woods, state parks, fishing, sailing, hunting, hiking, places to ride and ski and swim —but how many people who live in town really take advantage of all this?

"I think the chance to be able to do it," he replied, "and not do it, is a hell of a lot better than not doing it because you are not able to do it."

•   •   •

"The forthcoming Skimobile Rally raises the question of whether the town needs it. Although it may be of some advantage to the local motel business, its effect on 'the quality of life' of residents in the nearby area, as well as on local wildlife, is dubitable. . . ."

"The forthcoming Skimobile Rally raises the question of whether the town needs weekend residents to tell us what our town needs. Almost any winter evening from within my home I can hear and sometimes see six or eight skimobile enthusiasts enjoying the great outdoors. They are all good citizens that are having a little fun after a hard day's work. . . ."

LETTERS TO THE EDITOR

•   •   •

Some people here have no end of fun. Their life is busy, interesting, stimulating. It helps to have spending money, of course, but even those of modest means make use of the almost endless possibilities for leisure-time pursuits, for the fullness of the good life. And yet, for all too many, a small town is a place where there is "nothing to do." No excitement. No bright lights. Just the same old routine, the same faces and the annoying awareness that everyone knows it when you step out of line. There is too little variety, "no one to meet," "no place to go." As one lady put it: "If you're the mother of a teen-age boy or girl, this town is a desert." Some say that it helps account for the drinking problems in the community. And other embarrassments.

•   •   •

"This town? I'd say we're just as immoral as any place else. In other words, we're just as moral. We have some isolated cases of what might have been called real sinning some years ago, but we don't seem to speak about sin any more. I do know of some people here, some families, who could make Peyton Place look like wonderland."

•   •   •

"I really don't think there's been any real change in morality over the years in the town. You have the same sort of thing going on year after year—some old liaisons that everyone knows about. So it's not just a wild-young-bunch kind of thing. Perhaps it was done more discreetly in the past, but that's the only difference. People are really pretty tolerant. We've had some increase in homosexuals. Some gay couples—at least four I know of. But they're left alone. I don't think it would have been the same years ago."

•   •   •

"Our morals are just the same as ever. Human nature's been exactly the same for centuries. It's just that people talk more frankly these days about things which would have horrified people of my generation. Gee whiz, if I could tell you about the incest that went on right in this neighborhood. And families with illegitimate children. These things were done, but it was all suppressed and whispered around."

•   •   •

"If you want my opinion about immorality, I would say I'm against it."

•   •   •

Judging by the reputation small towns have had for straight-laced and narrow-minded opinions on moral matters, this has to be called a tolerant, forgiving and perhaps even sophisticated community. The inevitable transgressions that might have fired up the preachers in the past and set off a storm of indignant tongue-clucking, seem to be viewed by most people these days with bemused disinterest. The rumor mill still operates, but no one is run out of town. No one complains when the library buys *Portnoy's Complaint* or other works that might be considered pornographic, perhaps because the good ladies of the book-selection committee endeavor, as they have explained, to "pass up books whose only attraction appears to be their shock value." Some of the magazines and paperbacks sold on Main Street, like some of the films that appear at nearby cinemas, are so sexually explicit that they might once have provoked cries of outrage and threats of boycott, but there is no visible concern today and no evidence of harm done. It appears that people are not easily shocked. The prevailing attitude approximates the view of the English duchess who declared that she did not care what people did so long as they did not do it in the streets and frighten the horses.

· · ·

"Not too long ago we had one man in town who was a great reprobate. He had a terribly sweet wife, was very strict with his children and brought them up beautifully, but he had a great reputation. Galfriends located all over. But what lifted many eyebrows was the fact that he had his mistress living in the house right next door, and everybody knew it. It's a wonder he got away with that, but he did."

· · ·

"I suppose it can happen anywhere, but you hear stories going around about certain couples. It is said to be a 'known fact' that they are swapping wives. But it just isn't true at all. I was supposed to be one of the wives, and it's the last thing I'd ever do.

I just think people say this kind of thing out of jealousy. They just hate seeing people getting together and enjoying themselves."

• • •

"When I was growing up here, about 15 years ago, we used to have square dances in the Community House every other Saturday night. I'd walk all the way down the mountain, into the village, and all the way home again, a lot of miles, but it was worth it. Some of the wise guys would pass around a bottle, down in the basement, and the girls . . . well, we weren't as innocent as people thought. But now they're all respectable housewives."

• • •

"This is a well-behaved town today. In my early days there were a lot more drunks. During Prohibition everybody and his brother drank. There were stills all over town, and you could buy bootleg liquor right in the village."

• • •

"We were dry here even after Prohibition ended—straight through the war and into the 1950s. People took the train down to the next town if they wanted to buy a drink. Coming back on the local, they'd be too drunk to know where to get off. The conductor would tap 'em on the shoulder and push 'em off the train."

• • •

"Many years ago there was a fancy iron fence around St. Andrew's, like the one that's still there by the cemetery. One of our local characters was a little worse for wear on a certain Sunday morning. He was hanging on to the fence, practically falling across it. A friend came along and asked him, 'Going to church?' He raised up his head and said, 'Well, maybe. I'm sort of leaning that way.'"

• • •

SIXTY-SIX DAYS BEFORE ARRIVAL OF SPRING

HEADLINE

• • •

The Schaghticoke Slyders, who have established club rules "pertaining to use of snowmobiles in public places so as not to reflect unfavorably on the reputation of the club," have had their rally. Forty-five contestants from around the state turned up; more might have attended if there had not been foul-weather forecasts. The town survived.

• • •

Winter and summer, then, were two hostile lives, and bred two separate natures. Winter was always the effort to live; summer was tropical license. Whether the children rolled in the grass, or waded in the brook, or swam in the salt ocean, or sailed in the bay, or fished for smelts in the creeks, or netted minnows in the salt-marshes, or took to the pine-woods and the granite quarries, or chased muskrats and hunted snapping-turtles in the swamps, or mushrooms or nuts on the autumn hills, summer and country were always sensual living, while winter was always compulsory learning. Summer was the multiplicity of nature; winter was school.

HENRY ADAMS, *The Education of Henry Adams*

• • •

This household's morning routine. The clock-radio wakes us up at six. It is dark outside, cold in the bedroom. We close the window, turn up the thermostat and listen to the news and weather reports while we dress. If fresh snow has fallen heavily during the night we turn to a regional station to see whether the schools have been declared closed. While Leslie makes sure the children are awake and starts breakfast, I put on a jacket, cap and gloves and stomp through the drifted snow to the barn to feed the horses their hay and grain. It is desperately cold and bleak, but the inside of the barn is agreeable; the horses have been giving off body heat through the night. They kick at the sides of their stalls to tell me to get on with the job.

Then back at the house to join the family at the breakfast table. We keep an eye out for the headlights of the school bus as it labors up the mountain. There is a last-minute scramble for coats, boots, books and lunch bags. The driver is a pleasant man, a fellow deacon of the church, who waits patiently as the children slip and slide down to the road. While Leslie goes out to the barn to groom the horses and let them out for the day, I linger over coffee, reading yesterday's newspaper and thinking that I will get to work any minute now, but not yet.

•   •   •

"When I was growing up as a boy, back before World War One, it was mandatory in my house every November to have a barrel of flour, a barrel of sugar, 50 pounds of brown sugar, 25 cords of wood, a barrel of kerosene, plus all of the three hogs we butchered—the hams, the bacons, the spare ribs; everything but the squeal. That was customary to have everything we needed for the wintertime, because we didn't get to the village more than twice a year, once for election and once for taxes. And mother always had 200 quart jars of fruits and things downcellar—preserves and bins of potatoes and apples. And I mustn't leave out the barrel of cider. Every country home had one or two barrels of cider. And we always had a deer if we could get it. Neighbors would bring in things as well. We had all the fish trout we wanted out of a brook. And in very cold weather in April, when the brooks were running with ice-cold waters, we could get suckers with hard and firm flesh. Good eating. That's what we had on my farm. We worked hard, but it was a good life."

•   •   •

"Before electricity, people would shut up the rooms in winter and practically live in the kitchen. They had a stove or fireplace

in the front room, but they didn't go in there very much. The
bedrooms were cold. Some people would only heat up the
kitchen."

• • •

"People who use electric freezers today forget that we used to
have frozen food too. They'd butcher a cow or a pig or some animal and take it out to the barn. They'd put it on a pulley block,
pull it up and let it freeze up. Once a week they'd lower it down
and saw off what they wanted."

• • •

The latest Grand List property figures show that the town is
still growing, but at a nice leisurely pace. The total value is now
$12,501,298, a rise of $218,465 in a year's time. A dozen houses
have been added, giving us 814. We still have only the three small
factories, but nonresidential buildings now number 301, an increase of eight. We have 15 more motor vehicles (1,460 altogether), six more horses (148) and 41 more cattle (521), but we
still have the same number of sheep and goats (34), and we are
down from 31 swine to 20.

• • •

By one measurement the town has grown by only 60 cents in a
year's time. We impose a real estate conveyance tax of $1.10 on
every thousand dollars paid in property transfers. Total annual
transfers have been on the order of $1,758,500. The year before
last, the tax realized was $1,933.80. Last year: $1,934.40.

• • •

We worry about church attendance. It has been dwindling in so
many small communities, except for the fundamentalist sects, that
there has been a trend toward the use of theologically trained
lawyers, teachers and other professionals as part-time ministers.

"The people just don't concern themselves with religion any more," says one older woman, noting the empty pews and the few youth.

"The attendance figures indicate a general apathy toward religion," writes a boarding-school student who has done a careful survey of our religious scene.

And yet, as my wife points out (she heads the music committee at Congregational), "There is more to religion than going to church. Perhaps the emphasis is shifting from formal Sunday services to social-action Christianity throughout the week." This would seem to be what our preacher has in mind when he says, at the close of Sunday worship: "And now the service begins. Let us all go into all the world with love and courage. . . ."

·   ·   ·

The Catholic Sacred Heart Church, predictably enough, has the largest attendance: about 275, including many from nearby towns, between the two Sunday masses (three in the summer to accommodate vacationers). About half the Episcopalian voting members normally attend the Sunday services at St. Andrew's, but this is only a portion of the total flock. A number, however, go to the boarding-school chapels. The typical gathering at the First Congregational Church is about 40 to 50, roughly a quarter of the resident members and a sixth of the full membership. The handsome old Protestant churches fill up only during the Easter and Christmas seasons and at memorial services and other social occasions.

All in all, it is a poor showing in comparison to the days of religious zeal in the last century but a far healthier state of affairs than in the 1930s and 1940s when only eight or ten or twelve people might show up at Congregational for Sunday worship. It was a mission church in those lean days, receiving money from the outside, whereas today, after some 20 years of steady revival, the church supports missions elsewhere, conducts a lively Sunday school and attracts enough churchgoers to give at least the appearance of permanence.

But there is concern about the future. Can this church or any other church attract and hold spiritually hungry young people who seem to be seeking something more committed and Christlike than a ritualized, lukewarm Christianity?

• • •

Still, beyond the Sunday services, the churches here remain influential and, in some vital ways, virtually irreplaceable in the lives of the townspeople. As it was in the beginning, so today they are the town's beating heart, even though it beats faintly. "You can't help but feel that there is something good and lasting about a town whose tallest buildings are church towers," someone said. Even the citizen who rarely darkens the doorway of his church may well contribute to its support, enroll his children in the Sunday school, endorse the church-oriented youth activities, applaud the minister's work with the town's social agencies and turn to the church on family occasions of birth, marriage and death.

• • •

"One of the interesting things about this town is that from way, way back the three churches got on very well. They all supported each other's things. If there was a supper in the Congregational church or St. Andrew's, the Catholics would come to it, and vice versa. There's always been an easy interchange, which is unusual. An easy give-and-take. In some ways it's even improved, as the Catholic group has come up in the world and gained power. You start out with a salt-of-the-earth Irishman working on other people's farms, and now his descendants are prosperous businessmen."

• • •

The town is going through a very painful transition stage, where the old view of the Church is running directly up with the new view of the Church and its leaders. The young faculty members, the "non-natives," and the ministers are constant reminders of the new way. Many have fought fiercely against the new tide, and many are still fearful of losing the only security they have in such a fast moving world. They hate to see the Church move out of its sterile sphere, and cling fiercely to the old forms and old beliefs.

STUDENT'S SURVEY

• • •

"In a world so changing all the time, the church is the only basic and solid thing we have to hang on to."

• • •

"I like our priest. When he meets you on the street he talks about things in general. He doesn't ask why you didn't show up for mass last Sunday."

• • •

"The kids like the minister because he doesn't talk about religion all the time."

• • •

"You asked about the minister's role. I'm very pleased to be a part of a community where I can be of some real use as a minister. I'm very much involved in and able to have some influence in a whole range of things I might miss out on if I were in the suburbs. For example, last week I went to court twice, out of town, talking to lawyers and the bailiff and generally helping out a couple of local people. I was asked to go up to the state trooper's barracks in the middle of the night on some problem. It helps to make it a seven-day, day-and-night job, but it is satisfying to me to become that intimately involved in real human problems. As a matter of fact, the Congregational church has always been caught up in the affairs of the town. There's been a strong social-mindedness. So in order for me even to be involved with my people I have to be involved in these things outside the church.

"And that's fine! But the trouble is, I like preaching too—it's a discipline to put your thoughts in order, not just for the Sunday service but to give me the means to really help and inform people. The easiest thing for a minister to preach on is something obvious like the brutality of war or racial prejudice, but you've got to do a lot of work to preach on those real integral things that are bothering the people right in front of you. Loneliness, for example, or the way people talk without really saying anything or hear without really listening; I once gave a sermon on 'The Sound of Silence,' The Simon and Garfunkel record. I like to spend a third of my time on sermons, but there are so many people coming in all the time, and calls to make, and an amazing amount of pressure. It's almost impossible to relax or really concentrate on one thing. It bothers me immensely when I'm not doing a good job on my sermons, and of course it's no encouragement to talk to empty pews."

•   •   •

"A small-town minister doesn't have the same identity problem he would face in a larger community where there are so many different experts. Some ministers have a terrible identity problem. Their question is, What's a minister supposed to do? Just preach the word of God? In a large community with professional social workers, psychiatrists, doctors of every kind, professional organizations, what's the minister's job? Where does he fit in when Sunday stops and Monday begins? But a preacher here is basically a social worker, psychiatrist, general practitioner and man of God all put together. He's in on all the problems. I suppose, one way and another, that this has been true throughout the history of the town."

•   •   •

It is said the pioneers located on East Mountain, directly back of what now is called Good Hill. If so, they soon moved down and occupied Good Hill and Flanders. The "Great Plain" was thought to be swampy and worthless: it was near the Indians, too, who hunted over it at will. There is a tradition that Daniel Comstock, while out hunting, fell in with the Indian chief and treated him to "fire-water." This was the beginning of a friendship of great value to the whites. Comstock put up a building on the site of the present Botsford Fuller house, which served as store, dwelling house, and church. The store and dwelling apartments were on the first floor, and overhead was the one large room which was used for a "meeting house." The Indians came to trade their furs for rum, beads, and other articles that took their fancy, and Comstock taught them the gospel. In the upper room the Indians were gathered, and there the white man first worshipped. There, it is supposed, Robert Silliman preached, Cyrus Marsh was ordained, and the church was organized: and there they worshipped until 1743.

THE REVEREND BENJAMIN M. WRIGHT, PASTOR
FIRST CONGREGATIONAL CHURCH, 1889–96

•   •   •

In the early settlement days, when the townspeople were genuinely God-fearing and religion was a dominating fact of life, church and town were inseparable. And the church, for a long time, was exclusively the Congregational church. As mentioned earlier, two of the original fifty-three rights or shares of the township were reserved, according to the Act, "for the use of the ministry forever of the church established by the law of this government . . . and for the first Gospel minister settled as aforesaid." From the first, all divided lands were taxed fourpence an acre for the support of the ministry. The calling of a minister and the building of a meetinghouse were town business. Town meetings were constantly taking up church matters. Six gallons of rum, for example, were voted for the raising of a meetinghouse, and a year later the townspeople voted to clapboard the simple log building. The pastor was a politician too, and the Reverend Cyrus Marsh served the town for five terms as representative to the state General Assembly.

"The young church almost immediately had a case of discipline on its hands and heart," according to Francis Atwater's history of the town. "A member was tried and found guilty of the sin of drunkenness, and accordingly suspended until such time as he should make gospel satisfaction. This he did in a short time, and was restored to full communion."

A 25-year-old Yale graduate named Joel Bordwell succeeded Cyrus Marsh in 1758 and served as pastor for 53 years until his death in 1811. The 14-year-old girl, Jane Mills, whom he married soon after settling here, eventually bore him nine children. Although the money she brought to the marriage made him "one of the wealthiest clergymen in Connecticut," according to the Yale Annals, he followed the practice of other ministers by farming when not preaching. In addition he tutored boys preparing for college.

Many pastors have served the Congregational church since the Bordwell half-century. They were men of varying talents and temperaments, some provoking controversy (such as the Reverend Laurens P. Hickok, 1823–29), some calming troubled waters, some clinging to established forms, some searching and experimenting. "My predecessor," says our present young pastor, "went down to Selma and marched, and so forth, but his style of ministry was a bit different from mine, in the sense that he wore a collar and had more of a piety image. My style is more informal. I don't wear a collar, and I don't feel my strengths are in the area of piety. I like to think I'm the kind of guy you feel easy talking to."

•   •   •

The six years of Mr. Hickok's ministry were somewhat stormy, and the church and society records would lead one to think unsatisfactory. This, however, is untrue with regard to the church as a whole. As a preacher Mr. Hickok was simple, direct, and forceful, and as a man altogether lovable. All the trouble came from the violent dislike of the minister on the part of an influential man in the community, who permitted no opportunity for stirring up strife to pass. The minister was charged with unministerial conduct, such as whistling, vaulting fences, running on the streets, and driving a fast horse. Consociation was called, and it was decided that there was no cause for uneasiness, and therefore no reason for the dissolution of the pastoral relation. When, however, the call came from Litchfield inviting Mr. Hickok to succeed Dr. Lyman Beecher, he gladly availed himself of it as offering a solution of the difficulty, and thus the town lost the most eminent man who has ever occupied her pulpit.

FRANCIS ATWATER

• • •

The Congregational dominance of the town's religious landscape ended a good many decades ago as the Episcopalians and Roman Catholics increased in numbers and as the grip of the church on its members slipped. St. Andrew's is the result of the missionary labors of the Reverend Solomon Palmer, a former Congregational minister in a neighboring town, who resigned his pastorate, went across the ocean to be ordained in the Church of England and returned as a representative of the Society for the Propagation of the Gospel in Foreign Parts.

At that time, the town's few Church of England worshipers were obliged to meet in private homes. Public services had for years been forbidden by law; the New England settlers were almost exclusively dissenters from the doctrine and worship of the Church of England. The Reverend Palmer set about building a formal congregation, but it was his successor, the Reverend Richard Samuel Clarke, who first preached in the original church, erected a few years before the Revolutionary War. Its construction was the work of a prominent layman named Reuben Swift. Because "a contention of a private nature" arose in 1767, according to a history, "Swift and his family became Episcopalians and he built a small church, principally at his own expense."

The young church soon fell on dark days. The building eventually became the town hall. Throughout the Colonies, the revolution forced the closing of many Episcopalian churches. Some of the clergy withdrew to England, and loyalists were silenced or driven away. The Episcopalians made a comeback after the war, however. An Episcopal Society was legally formed here in 1808, and the dynamic Reverend George B. Andrews came to town a decade later to preach at the makeshift St. John's church. "The congregation at this place," said the bishop, soon afterward, "seems to be rising from the state of depression into which it has languished." When the present stone church was built in 1827, it was named after the Apostle St. Andrew as a way of honoring the good Reverend Andrews.

Today, with the addition of the two boarding-school parishes, the Episcopalians outnumber the Congregationalists. The Catholics, steadily increasing in numbers, influence and affluence, still worship in the same little Sacred Heart Church, dedicated in 1884. They have only recently become a full-fledged parish after a long history as a mission.

There is a synagogue in the next town to the south and churches for Lutherans, Methodists, Baptists, Presbyterians and Christian Scientists within half an hour's drive. There are Mormons and Seventh Day Adventists in our midst, too. They occasionally stop by at the house to spread the faith.

*   *   *

In the 1840s and '50s, there were a goodly number of Millerites in town. They preached the Second Coming of Christ and expected the end of the world. They believed prophecies would be fulfilled upon a certain day. Accordingly, on that date, they all dressed in white robes and at evening spent the time in the fields ready to greet the Lord when he came. In their ecstasy many climbed trees, poised along the branches ready to take their flight into the heavens. Along toward dawn a neighbor's boy, no doubt an unbeliever, called out, "Here He comes!" The minister and other men of the group, when they found it a false report, chased the boy but didn't catch him. "The spell was broke," and they all went home to await another revelation of THE day.

HISTORICAL SOCIETY FILES

*   *   *

February 25. Five o'clock in the afternoon. Sitting at my desk, I feel a sudden warmth on my back. The room begins to glow. I swivel my chair around and see through the west window the brilliant setting sun bursting through the clouds and igniting the millions of tiny icicles on the trees and bushes. It is sparkling, dazzling, heart-stoppingly beautiful. An explosion of diamonds.

• • •

The Episcopal minister has resigned. He has had a frustrating experience, in the four years he has been at St. Andrew's, trying to introduce changes and move people to his way of thinking. On the other hand, as some of his flock are quick to say (often with a startling lack of charity), "this bearded young man with his new-fangled ideas stirred up a lot of trouble." He posed a threat to the security of tradition which comforts the set-in-their-ways church-goers. "And, besides, he didn't make enough calls on shut-ins." Some people took to staying away from church entirely.

• • •

"It has been an unhappy and confusing time. I'm afraid some of us gave the minister a very rough time even though he had a lot of devoted supporters. People forgot that he was only following the bishop's orders. Episcopal churches are being reformed all over the country so that we can keep our young people and really mean something in this crazy world. That was his job when he came here, and that's what he tried to do. But, first of all, you have this tight-Yankee attitude about spending money. Good Lord! We'd been talking and nit-picking for years about fixing up the church! And then, remember, people in an old New England town like to do things themselves in their own good time, not have things done *to* them. And they felt very comfortable with the 'thees' and 'thous' and the beautiful old language in the old Prayer Book. We started using the 'trial liturgy' three years ago, but we made the mistake of calling it the 'New Liturgy.' People got upset, you wouldn't believe it! No wonder the minister became discouraged. Now, for the present anyway, we've gone back to the old liturgy."

•   •   •

The minister was very popular until he suggested changing the service to the New Liturgy, and remodeling the interior of the church, which hit many in a very sensitive spot. However, he did a good job of gauging church opinion before he made the changes. Many who are against him will deny that he consulted the congregation, but he did, by holding discussion groups, and voting sessions. He had the church remodeled very attractively, which now people will admit is a great improvement, but the response to the New Liturgy was not very favorable. He used the new service every Sunday. Many people in interviews said that they did not mind the New Liturgy once a month or so, but did not like it "jammed down our throats."

STUDENT'S SURVEY

•   •   •

I remember the minister telling me, months ago, that "there has been a strong reaction to the new things that have been happening in the Episcopal church over the last few years. Some new things liturgically. Some people don't see the need for the new communion service. They are reluctant to recognize that *the* service in the Episcopal church is the communion service. They see religion as a very personal thing. They go to church not to be concerned about other people who are there but to seek some kind of spiritual refreshment on their own. I find all this extremely frustrating when I theologically consider the church as a community. I get annoyed by people who can sit next to someone else in church for an hour on a Sunday and then the next day deal with him without any sense of Christian charity. It should be a Christian relationship on a day-to-day 24-hour basis. I've been criticized by some of the older people for harping on this: that they should be involved with each other in many respects; that there should be a sense of community within the church. Our New Liturgy tries to encourage human contacts by having peo-

ple turn to each other during the service, shaking hands or em-
bracing or something like this. It is a restoration of the ancient
kiss of peace but in a modern form. Many people were absolutely
appalled at the idea of doing this. It was a very stilted thing at
first, but we're doing it. Even within families you can see that
there is a freer expression than before, but some of the old-timers
would try to find out beforehand whether we were doing the
New Liturgy or the old Prayer Book and stay away if it was the
New Liturgy."

• • •

"Listen, this is *New England!* We're a little cold sometimes. It
takes us a while to warm up to strangers, and I'm not sure that
we want to get too close to each other."

• • •

In all three of our churches there is a basic tug-of-war between
the traditionalists and modernists, and not only on questions of
ritual but on the church's role in the hurly-burly of the everyday world. The high-attendance Sacred Heart Church is the
least active, socially and politically, but its modernized services
are relaxed, using a simplified version of the traditional forms. Although many have been reluctant to accept the New Liturgy, the
controversy has been muted locally because the basic decisions
were made in the higher reaches of the Roman Catholic Church.
There is a popular view that "clergy belong in the pulpits, not
leading marches and demonstrations," yet talks with town Catholics reveal a strong sentiment in favor of the Church's playing an
active role in everything from racial and poverty problems to
family planning.

The two Protestant churches go through greater agonies as
they decide how much to involve themselves in contemporary
issues. The Congregationalists, even though they are hard-pressed
to raise their $20,000 operating budget (including the minister's
$6,700 salary), contribute an additional $3,500 for "Christian Out-

reach" purposes, ranging from the support of missionaries in central Africa to aid to children in Hong Kong and on the Sioux Indian reservation in South Dakota. Some churchgoers make it clear they would rather pay such "conscience money" than sit through sermons on the problems themselves. According to one woman, "People want to be lifted up, not let down."

• • •

"In St. Andrew's, anyway, the reaction to a sermon on social justice or some other contemporary issue is sometimes extremely controversial. There are a lot of people, especially younger ones and the schoolmasters, who want things like this. I would say an absolute majority. But some of the older people become upset, and I think that's understandable. The church has always been a bastion of security for them, and they hate to see it change."

• • •

The Church and politics should be separate. The Church in general should be concerned with its parishioners, their lives, their children, and to keep our faith in God. The wars and civil rights and other things should be outside our Church. I feel the traditional prayers and creeds should always stay as they were in the beginning. In a world so changing all the time it is the only basic and solid thing to hang on to. I feel our Church is changing not for the good of the people. Sometimes I'm ashamed of the things our Rectors are doing to our Church. In a town as small as this the Rector should know each and every one of his flock and to see their needs. These days the Rectors feel they should sit and the flock should go to them. Life does not work that way.

LETTER FROM "A MOTHER"

• • •

"We get so much news about war and crime and poverty and race on the television news that we get upset hearing about it in church on Sunday."

• • •

"Probably I'm too conservative, but it really bothers me just hearing the preacher use the word 'abortion' in church."

•   •   •

"People get it into their heads that I devote every sermon to some social issue. Not at all. But it seems to happen that the fellow who stays away from church because I talked about race problems one Sunday is sure to return, months later, on the very day I mention race again."

•   •   •

"Even in Sunday school we get complaints about being too relevant. One woman said that the trouble with the curriculum is, there's not enough Bible. I said there's a lot of Bible in the instruction, and I said I have a book here which says which passages are recommended in each course. Then she said that the real trouble is, they're always trying to *relate* the Bible!"

•   •   •

"Our preacher at Congregational has preached about abortions, gun control, the death penalty, racial problems, war, politics, pollution, prison conditions, all these problems you see in the headlines—not all the time, mind you, but just often enough to disturb the people who simply come to church to feel closer to God and who don't want to have to think about anything. Well, there are ministers all over the country preaching the same word from the pulpit and getting into hot water. Sometimes there are enough reactionaries around to boot them right out. But there's something about our church; I guess we either have more tolerant conservatives or there are more liberal tendencies than you'd suspect. For example, the minister polled the basic churchgoers—about 70 out of the 300 members, the ones who try to get to the Sunday services, though they don't always make it—and there was a really amazing majority, more than three quarters, in favor of the church being involved in racial problems, political legislation and so on.

In an earlier poll, he asked whether the church should play a role in sex education for our kids. Well, there were 50 in favor, only two against, and the rest unsure. I think that's fantastic!

"One important factor in all this, of course, is that we have a minister who may have some radical ideas, at least in contrast to what people are used to, and who experiments with different forms of worship, but he succeeds because he doesn't offend people with superficial things. He doesn't have long hair or dress or behave like a revolutionary. He's enough of a diplomat to get a lot of people involved in these decisions—the deacons, the committees, the 'coffee hour' discussions after the Sunday service—so that the changes come in gradually with a lot of support. Also, and this is really important, he makes the calls on the sick and the old people, he's involved in FISH and the Social Service Committee, he does tremendous work with the youth, and he's always willing to listen to people. He knows there's been criticism. The old-timers in a small-town church can be very hard on a young minister coming in from the outside. But he takes account of these feelings. The result is a good all-around relationship and a church that's willing to be involved in the real problems of the world."

• • •

A flu epidemic is upon us. People are complaining of aches, pains, chills, fever and chest congestion. School absenteeism is soaring. Kids all over town are home in bed. The two doctors are swamped with calls. We learn from the state Department of Health that we are suffering from a foreign invader known as "Massachusetts B."

• • •

It has been a grumpy, perplexing winter so far. Uncertain of itself. Sometimes achingly cold yet not inclined to heap a vast amount of snow on us. We have had early and frequent temperamental outbursts but no forceful follow-through. All too often wet winds have glazed the surface of the snow, or scoured the high ground, making it difficult to roam our mountain on cross-country skis. It almost makes us long for the great winter of a couple of years back when an early February snowstorm brought us three feet of snow—and many a snowdrift that went above our heads. It was said to be the equal of the Great Blizzard of 1888. The schools were closed for days, and it took the town crew and volunteers a long time to clear a single lane on Skiff Mountain Road. Many lesser roads were blocked for days longer. Travelers were stranded and cars were buried. Some shopkeepers went to work on skis. A few people took to going to the village on horseback. Our insurance man, just up the road, set off for Main Street on skis and disappeared for so long that the firemen and other volunteers had a major rescue operation going before he finally emerged from the drifts of the river road late at night.

•   •   •

"Records have fallen right and left," say the local editors, who patrol their outdoor thermometer. "Old-timers figure there must have been a winter as rugged as this, but nobody can remember when." One day the temperature fell to 16 below zero. For the first 35 days of the year, according to a local calculator, it has been 260 degrees below normal.

•   •   •

MAIN STREET PROFILE CHANGED.
SEVERAL DYING MAPLES
ARE FELLED THIS WEEK

HEADLINE

•   •   •

Instant welfare. A friend telephones. He is surveying the deacons to see if the preacher can go ahead and give $100 to a local woman who needs money for legal assistance immediately.

Agreed.

•   •   •

It occurs to me, as we import people who are trying to get away from the problems of the world, that our relatively trouble-free condition is due in some measure to our way of exporting problems. Because we are small, we can shuffle off quite a few of our woes to larger neighboring towns and the cities. Since we have no jail, hospital, mental institution, drug rehabilitation center, unemployment office, welfare agency, or whatever, we shift out of town and out of sight a number of the sick and indigent, the delinquent, the unemployed, the mentally ill and other problem cases that we sometimes think are peculiar to cities.

• • •

"We have social problems all right. Hard to say whether that makes us the typical American town, or what, but you might say that we're only human. We've got a number of problem families, the names that keep coming up before the Social Service Board. The ministers, the selectmen, the doctors, the school principal, the visiting nurse, the state trooper—they meet once a month at the Center School and cross-pollinate the problems. It's a kind of exchange of information. You can find out why this kid in school comes in with smelly clothes and no bath. It turns out there's no running water in the house. Or there's been some big blow-up in the family. There are problems of poverty, drinking, drugs, too many children, not enough to eat, people sleeping around, children neglected, father beating up his kid, people in and out of the mental hospitals all the time. But the good side of all this is that the town isn't running away from these problems. The ministers, the town officials, the Social Service Board—these people are concerned and very much involved. We take care of our own."

• • •

FISH has been operating in the town for several years now. We are fundamentally a group of people who wish to show our concern, through action, for our neighbors in need. Anyone may call upon FISH for assistance and anyone may be a member. There is never any charge for any service the FISH provides. If we can help, it's our privilege. We are untrained ordinary people who will try to be a good neighbor to you. When one calls the FISH number, a 24-hour answering service will put you in touch with a member of the FISH.

ANNOUNCEMENT

•   •   •

"What you get here is an immediate community response to problems. If there is a fire or a flood or some old lady needs to be taken to the hospital, we move fast and take care of the problem. But these are responses to emergency problems, not to existing problems. Existing problems are hard to move because they are there and they've been there a long time. Suppose a family is living in pretty miserable conditions; we are inclined not to interfere. The independent New England spirit is there, you know. We figure it's their own fault if that's the way they live. But if there's an emergency and they need help, we give it.

"You have the same response to improvements like the sewer, a new school or something like this new building code which a lot of people are against because it's coming down on us from the top, the state. If we have to expand the school because we've got so many new kids, people will say, 'Why can't the kids squeeze up a bit? Can't we just use the same facilities? When I went to school we didn't have all these luxuries! What's the big emergency?'

"You especially find resistance like this in a small New England town which is used to holding its own purse strings and handling its own functions. There's resistance to anything that comes down from above, like the sewer which the state says we've got to have, because they think we're polluting the river. People write into the paper and say it's un-American."

•   •   •

"Have you noticed how many wives have more education than their husbands? And how many women are working? It makes a really serious problem in some families. The wife has been somewhat submissive to her husband over the years, even though she may have had more schooling, because he expects to run things. She's just the little housewife. But then the children grow up, and she gets a job or gets more education. Or she's been doing more reading than he has and taking part in various town affairs. You have many more women doing social things than the men. She begins to feel her oats! There is a social-mindedness that women get. Then they go home, and the husband isn't interested. If he's an average working man who likes to watch football games on television and she becomes a schoolteacher who is very socially aware, there's a danger she will look down on him. He will feel he has lost command of the situation at home. Maybe it's women's liberation, but it spells trouble."

•   •   •

"A huge percentage of the divorce problems I know about—including people who are getting along so badly that they are on their way to breaking up—have been at the root bottom an education difference between husband and wife. Often the husband never realizes how bad the situation is until the wife walks out on him, or almost does. He gets depressed, gets a few drinks under his belt, and then they're either in for real trouble or they get up the courage to call the minister or someone to help them out. One great thing here is that you do have some very capable and sympathetic people you can turn to."

•   •   •

Old annual reports of the town reveal that the down-and-out have always been with us and that their basic needs were met. Small amounts of money, food and clothing were provided to both the "town poor" and the "outside poor." In 1909 the selectmen spent $664 caring for the town poor, including a $16.50 payment to E. W. Bull for lodging 55 tramps, and $3.95 to Watson & Morehouse's General Store for providing "shirts, etc." to one Ransom Hurd.

•   •   •

"We have an item in the selectmen's budget called 'Outdoor Relief.' We agree to operate and follow the state's book. We use their application forms and follow their rules for determining welfare eligibility. Under that, so long as we do it their way, they will reimburse us 75 percent of whatever we give out in welfare. But the way it's set up, we take care of most of the one-shot problems, and they take care of the ones that are continuing problems. So, to take an example: a woman recently separated from her husband had two little girls, and she applied for aid to dependent children, through the state. It takes the state machinery some time to turn around, investigate and so on. So if she had gotten into dire straits in the meantime, the First Selectman could have done something. Like pay the rent for a month and be reimbursed later. The selectmen actually do some things that don't show up in the relief budget at all. Unfortunately they chip away at the Highways General or something else. The men deliver the dead wood we cut down to various poor souls who can't get their own firewood. We think this is good work. One poor widow: we clean things out for her every so often—her stovepipe and so on. She'd probably end up a welfare case again if we didn't do this, so we just sort of go ahead. She works a little bit and earns just enough to get along on Social Security."

• • •

"Of course, this town was never a town of great wealth. Oh, we've always had people who were comfortably off. We would speak of people who had money as being 'very comfortable.' They would have money to invest in things, but nothing ostentatious. Money has been rather underplayed here."

• • •

"Let me contrast our small-town life with the suburbs I've lived in. I would say that most people, depending on their background, education, money, and so on, see people much like themselves in their primary relationships. The carpenters and painters get to-

gether, and the highbrows get together. But their periphery relationships seem deeper and wider here. You have a great many
associations with people outside your natural level or status. Also,
by being a person of real quality, you can earn a lot of respect in
all quarters. One man I like is a plain fellow who goes about in a
white T-shirt. He does a lot of things, like driving a school bus.
He used to have chickens and sheep, used to run an old people's
home, serves as a church deacon, and so on. He knows everyone,
talks to everyone in town, and everyone respects him. He gives
the impression that he doesn't have to tip his hat to anyone, and
that's true."

      •   •   •

More than any other expression, though, the people themselves . . .
like to use 'ordinary man' or 'average American' or 'plain person.'
Again and again one hears those words, all the time spoken with pride
and conviction and a touch of sadness, a touch of worry—as if the
country has not learned to appreciate such people, and maybe even
makes them pay for the sins of others, pay with their lives, their
savings, their energies. And they have indeed paid. They have seen
their savings mean less, or disappear, as inflation gets worse and worse.
They have had to take second jobs to keep up with prices. They have
sent their sons abroad, and thousands of them have died. . . .

ROBERT COLES, *The Middle Americans*

      •   •   •

"I work hard, and I pay my taxes. And there's nothing that gets
me madder than seeing these welfare people in the cities getting
handouts—from *my* tax money!—when they don't have the guts
to get out and work. I mean *any* kind of work! If a man doesn't
have pride in himself, then he's *nothing!*"

      •   •   •

There is not much tolerance here for loafers, unless they have
carved out a niche for themselves as authentic town characters,
and none at all for parasites. Although there is a hazy realization

that the great majority of the people on the nation's ballooning welfare rolls are not, in fact, able-bodied men, the typical working man in these parts has the distinct impression that he is supporting a vast army of "welfare bums," not to speak of college students who "riot, burn, complain and don't know when they're well off." All of this hurts, because he works hard and believes deeply, as well he should, that it is his kind of earnest labor which has made the country great. Although he may be better off today than ever before, life is still a struggle. "Things don't come easy," he will say. "Sometimes it seems like you have to run faster just to stay in the same place." He is making more money than ever, but he feels himself being pulled backward by taxes and the high cost of everything.

Very often his wife works for pay as well as himself, and he is likely to have some sort of second job. A small town offers a fair number of opportunities for making extra money at a part-time job or running a little business on the side.

• • •

"It's quite common in towns this size for a man to bury people as a sideline. The only thing is, it's gotten to be more complicated than in the old days. Our postmaster handles the funerals, but he leaves the embalming to an expert in another town. His grandfather, who used to run the funerals from his general store, was a funeral director, medical examiner, casket maker and embalmer, all combined. It was more common then to have the funeral service in your own home, but if they wanted to use the funeral director's house, he'd just haul out the living room furniture for as long as was required."

• • •

"People used to be content with a plain and simple funeral. Now they feel they have to put on a show. The trouble is, those who can least afford it are inclined to spend the most. Sometimes they come in and say there's $2,000 in the insurance money and they want a $2,000 funeral. I tell them they ought to spend only part of that on the funeral and use the rest to put a new roof on the house."

* * *

There is a Cemetery Association, which looks after the maintenance of our principal cemeteries, most of them fully occupied. The selectmen have just decided to augment the town grant to the association so that work can be done on relocating the dirt road running through the Congregational cemetery. That way, one more row of graves can be provided. We are said to be running out of room for the dead.

* * *

Last year the town had 20 marriages, 24 births and 33 deaths. The year before: 28 marriages, 23 births, 29 deaths. "People do seem to be dying a lot more these days," someone said, "but I guess the new families moving into town make up for it." One third of our inhabitants are under the age of 21.

* * *

"There aren't many of the old breed left. I mean the fellows who'd come down to the village, regular as clockwork, to the Grange and these other outfits. One fellow who's still with us, he never misses a Grange meeting. I remember one evening seeing his wife walking through the cut, across the river there, and I offered her a ride. 'Where's your husband?' I said. 'Well,' she said, 'he was ready and I wasn't, so he left.' They don't make them like that anymore."

* * *

We meet an out-of-town psychiatrist at a party. "You can find a lot of craziness in these towns," he says, "but at least there is a lot of room to be crazy in."

* * *

"There was one character we called 'Crowbar.' He used to say, 'I'll never die,' but he did."

. . .

"We've always had characters in this town. There's even a hermit someplace near you. Our number one character comes down the mountain with his dog and sort of floats around town, doing odd jobs when he feels like it, sitting in front of the stores, talking about the weather. You discover that he's a very knowledgeable man. A definite individualist. What gives me a kick is that he really *looks* like a character with his big beard and floppy hat.

"But I don't think we'll ever see the equal of Joel and Orinda Pratt. He was a great old guy who dealt in livestock and everything. He used to go up to Fort Ticonderoga and bring down cattle, all on his own. He lived with his sister Orinda. She was quite a woman. Graduated from Vassar College. He lived downstairs and she lived upstairs. They didn't get along. One day he took her to church and tried to charge her a quarter for the ride. Then she charged him for feeding him. After that he wouldn't take her to church, and she wouldn't feed him. He'd sit downstairs in a chair in front of an old stove and have a beam of some kind sticking into the fire. He'd just keep pushing it in as the end burned off."

. . .

According to a monograph written for the Historical Society, Joel Pratt was "probably the most unusual and most laughed at person in the town. He appeared to be ridiculous because he had some original ideas and followed them without caring how much people laughed at him or at the horse-and-ox team and other makeshifts he used. He was never well and strong. That was one reason he was such a poor farmer. He was not strong enough to work hard as most farmers do and he was too economical to hire good help. He went about in both summer and winter with many layers of clothing topped by an overcoat tied with a rope around the waist. 'What will keep out the cold,' he explained, 'will keep out the heat.' In hot weather he slept during the day and worked at night, mowing his fields in the moonlight while his neighbors slept."

As for sister Orinda, she was "an unforgettable character":

She had higher education but no common education. She could paint flowers beautifully but didn't know how to do a washing. She could make delicious candy but she couldn't cook. When she found a hen's nest with seventeen eggs in it she just put them all in a custard. It was a rocky custard.

To make a grammatical error was to her unpardonable. After a church service she would tell the minister of his grammatical errors or of any words he had mispronounced. She had excellent taste in dress but would dress so wildly around home she scared a new hired man. He thought she was some weird person, perhaps a witch or insane person. She called her brother's horse-and-ox team a novelty and bought many postcard pictures of him and the team to send to relatives.

She was up on the etiquette of polite society but knew nothing about the common courtesies. The ordinary thought her rude and impudent.

Words are inadequate.

.   .   .

The veterinarian has put a classified advertisement in the newspaper to announce that a certain lady in town "makes the best Apple Pie in the world!"

.   .   .

A local well driller reports that the artesian well he has been drilling for a new homeowner in Bog Hollow has come in with water pressure so great that it lifted 4,000 pounds of drilling rods and equipment right off the bottom. The overflow is estimated at over 300 gallons a minute or half a million gallons a day. A flat

stone was thrown into the well. Minutes later it was found floating near the surface.

•   •   •

Deacons meeting tonight. A number of serious things are discussed, particularly the booklet we are preparing to help the be-
reaved cope with the problem of a death in the family. But we
spend a few minutes on less-consequential matters. Someone has
objected to our new communion practice of offering large hand-
broken portions of freshly baked homemade bread, so that each
worshiper must tear off a morsel. Should we return to neatly seg-
mented cubes of sliced supermarket bread? Emphatically, no.
Someone else has complained about the noise in church when
members of the congregation place their tiny communion wine
cups in the holes in the wooden racks behind the pews. Should
we go to the trouble and expense of lining the little holes with
felt or plastic? Again, no.

•   •   •

We wake up in the small hours of the morning to discover that
fresh snow has fallen heavily on the land and sifted into the bedroom. Deep under the blankets, sublimely cozy, we hear the reassuring sounds of the town trucks scraping the snow off the road.

•   •   •

No one thought of clearing the roads in winter until very recent days.
If a man's horse could not get him and his sleds and sleighs out of the
farmyard, he was just out of luck. The first snowplow came to our
town in the age of Calvin Coolidge, in the winter of 1922–23. It and
its successors have revolutionized winter life.

LEWIS GANNETT, *Cream Hill*

•   •   •

"There is a time bomb ticking away in this town. I mean all that
riverfront property, about 1,500 acres, on both sides just north of

the village. It is owned by the Stanley Works, the big tool company in New Britain. That makes them the largest real estate owner in the town except for the state. When they bought the property more than sixty years ago they planned to dam it up and produce their own electricity. As it turned out, they got power from somewhere else, and they've just held on to this land ever since. Even with zoning there could be a lot of development there some-day which could either be good or bad for the town. Or else, if you believe the rumors, the whole area might be taken over by the power company."

•   •   •

I am sure that the businessmen and engineers in the power industry who have designed this project believe that it represents progress. Progress not only for the power business but for the people of this state as well. I am equally sure that none of these men is against beauty. So the question, I think, is how much landscape you are ready to destroy for how much progress.

I am not an engineer, and the only thing I know for sure about elec-tric power is that I pay for it every month. But I do know something about beauty; I think this is the most beautiful part of the world I have seen. And it would take an awful lot of progress to make me believe that what I see ought to be destroyed in order to bring that progress about.

ARTHUR MILLER

•   •   •

About a century ago, technological progress in the iron indus-try came along and did us the good turn of restoring the beauty and serenity of these hills. During the middle decades of the nine-teenth century, when this cluster of towns produced most of the nation's iron, it was, according to an area newspaper, "one of the most ruthlessly despoiled 'rural' areas in the country": a grimy, smoky region of company towns, cheap housing, foundries, sheds, car-wheel factories, ore pits, and mountains denuded of trees.

"The lovely winding dirt roads were practically choked with rumbling ore and charcoal wagons, not to mention dust and noise and certainly uncouth language."

When new methods of steelmaking made backcountry ironworks obsolete, the industry moved to Pittsburgh, Gary and other places far from New England. Nature came back into its own. The scars have been healed, as if by a green miracle.

Now progress is coming our way again, this time in some massive new forms that could ultimately undo nature's work of restoration. The state highway planners are aiming superhighways at our scenic townships from at least two directions. The promise—or threat—is that they will accelerate industrial and residential development. Half an hour's drive to the north, in a pretty little town with a population of less than a thousand, Northeast Utilities is planning to install one of the world's greatest pumpstorage hydroelectric plants. It is to be a $275-million, two-million-kilowatt project, which will have an immense social, economic and environmental impact on the surrounding region. A great reservoir will be created by the flooding of a pastoral valley. Another will be gouged out of an ecologically priceless mountaintop that happens to be the largest, most rugged and varied wilderness area in the state. (The two sites will account for one sixth of the entire township.) Ultimately, when all the facilities are installed, huge transmission towers will take giant steps across the countryside, carrying electricity to the masses of megalopolis.

• • •

In a separate electric-power development, beginning half an hour's drive to the south, 21 towns, including Arthur Miller's, are facing the prospect of transmission towers marching across seventy-five miles of rural landscape. The outraged cries of the townspeople are echoes of the painter Thomas Cole's lament to his merchant patron when the railroad invaded the Hudson Valley: "They are cutting down all the trees in the beautiful valley on which I have looked so often with a loving eye. Join me in maledictions on all dollar-godded utilitarians."

*   *   *

Conservationists, alarmed landowners and escapists from the world of tomorrow have launched a well-financed movement to head off the pump-storage project before it becomes a certainty. Their chances would have been slim only a few years ago, but the environmental movement has caught fire throughout the country. People in this region have begun to speak of it as a unique "eco-district." At the same time, however, there are numerous residents of that small town who welcome the power plant. They speak of work and business opportunities and the tax bonanza sure to result from the addition of something like $100 million to the present modest property tax roll of less than $8 million. The opposition warns that this is fool's gold and that a whole way of life may be destroyed by the six years of construction and by the forced growth of the town. Caught up in the middle are any number of uneasy and perplexed citizens. They would probably agree with the local farmer who said, "I don't say that I would like to see the valley flooded here, but if it's going to come, it's going to come, and nothing in God's world can stop it."

*   *   *

Here I live. After wandering, this valley is my home, this very hillside, these green acres. I want no other. This is my progress, the succession of the seasons; this is my reward, the product of the earth. Here may I think and love and work. Here have I lived and here I would die, for of all places under the sun I know of none that contents me better.
                    DAVID GRAYSON, *The Countryman's Year*

*   *   *

It appears that we have just barely escaped, at least for a while, the kind of massive intrusion which is in store for the people up the river. A few years ago, making a survey for Northeast Utilities, a Boston engineering firm advised that there were, in all Connecticut, two excellent sites for the creation of a mammoth pump-storage hydroelectric facility. One was the town that has been selected by the utility. The other was our town. Specifically, the pine swamp on Skiff Mountain, half a mile north of this house.

•   •   •

"Look, there's a tremendous demand for more electricity, and the population's growing all the time. There's a published projection of New England's power situation in 1990 which shows a one-million-kilowatt pumped-storage facility right in this town. They'd dam up the river and make a reservoir reaching back about five miles. And they'd dig a stupendous hole in that swamp on your mountain. Then they'd pump up the water during the off hours and shoot it down when there's a peak demand for electricity. People in the cities are already screaming for the stuff. It's got to come from somewhere, and one day we're going to be elected."

•   •   •

In our rush toward uniformity, in our effort to standardize everything from education to production, from life styles to death styles, perhaps there is no longer room for quirky, complex small towns. Perhaps—like the flivver and the butter churn—they have outlived their usefulness. Perhaps—like the bald eagle—they are fatally out of synch in this jet age where everyplace is as close as your airport and almost everyplace looks like everyplace else.
    PEGGY CLIFFORD AND JOHN M. SMITH, *Aspen: Dreams and Dilemmas*

•   •   •

An icy, brittle morning. After a freezing rain we live in a slippery, gleaming, glassy world—beautiful to behold but perilous. The house has a skin of ice. The winds shake jewels from the trees. The frozen grass, appearing in patches here and there, crackles as we walk.

•   •   •

We seem to be guaranteed at least one hot issue to see us through each cold winter. Last year we were agitated by the ski-area proposal. That one is in the courts now. Some of the land-owners near the proposed site are trying to block it by suing the town.

This one is about our 50 miles or so of old, neglected and for-gotten roads and whether we should formally declare them ex-tinct in order to avoid future road-building costs, which conceiv-ably could be as high as a million dollars. Some of our past and present officials warn that an individual or corporate developer could buy property next to one of our obsolete cow paths, prove that it was a road long ago and compel us to turn it into a proper modern thoroughfare at great expense.

(Years ago, when the small towns controlled the legislature, the state would pay the cost of any additional road mileage, but the urbanized General Assembly has decided to allocate its road grants on a population rather than a mileage basis. Now our town would have to raise its 2,000 population to 18,000 to qualify for increased state aid.)

Blanket abandonment of the old roads is proposed as the best way to get rid of this particular Pandora's box, but there is a lot of opposition. The retired roads serve us splendidly as backwoods trails for recreation—something not to be lightly discarded. Aban-donment would put the trails under the control of adjoining land-owners.

All of this was thrashed out at a well-attended town meeting last night, but many of us came away more confused than ever. Neither the town counsel nor any other legal expert could say for sure that we are obligated to revive an old road every time a land-owner insists on his rights. Each case would have to be examined individually. The meeting was adjourned until Saturday, when we will decide the issue on the voting machines.

· · ·

The warning for the town meeting was possibly the longest in our history because it listed every one of our existing roads. They include such intriguing names as Gay, Bacon and Cobble, Ore Hill, Bald Hill, Treasure Hill and Spooner Hill, as well as Flat Rock Road, which isn't flat, and Straight Road, which isn't straight.

• • •

We've been frozen up tight all winter, but now, as the days grow longer, we can hear a faint gurgling beneath the hard jacket of the stream. They say the ice on the river broke up last night. You can see the snow fading away and the hard ruts on the dirt roads turning mushy. March is the month for moisture. The brooks are rising and the forest trails are muddy. There are puddles in our leaky basement. Winter seems to be losing its grip. Spring is edging in.

• • •

The first sign of spring here is when the ice breaks up in the inkwell at the post office. A month later the ice leaves the lakes. And a month after that the first of the summer visitors shows up and the tax collector's wife removes the town records from her Frigidaire and plugs it in for the summer.

E. B. WHITE, *One Man's Meat*

• • •

The Board of Finance has recommended that the First Selectman's salary be raised by a thousand dollars to $9,500.

• • •

Result of the referendum: 242 voted to abandon the old roads, 125 voted No. The trouble is, however, that the selectmen are not at all happy about the decision, and two of them are advocating a do-nothing policy, even at the risk of infuriating some townspeople. It looks as though we'll be fussing about this issue for months to come.

• • •

The sap is flowing again in the sugar maples. The tapping season has begun. This is not exactly sugar bush country—we have nothing to equal the late-winter maple syrup industry of Vermont—but a number of our neighbors have buckets hanging from spouts poked into their trees, and I daresay we will take it up one day. The most impressive nearby operation is down in the woods behind one of the old Skiff farmhouses. We put on our boots, thick jackets and woolly caps and make our way to the old cabin, which is gushing steam through every pore. Like Finns stepping into the sauna, we leave the cold outdoors and approach the blazing fire and the hot evaporator, as big as a barn door. We look down on a boiling, sweet-smelling sea of foaming sap. Our friends are slowly filling up square-edged cans with fresh syrup. We go home with enough quarts to last us through a year of waffles and pancakes.

·   ·   ·

It is a lot of work for little reward. It takes more than 40 gallons of sap, which is mostly water, to make a single gallon of syrup, and if you lack an evaporator and try to do the sugaring off on the kitchen stove you run the risk of steaming off the wallpaper. From the tapping of the trees and the gathering of buckets and logs to the final flourish of candymaking by dripping syrup on the snow, it is a sweaty, laborious, time-consuming effort, but there are valuable intangible rewards. It is a whole-family project and a marvelously rounded, beginning-to-end manufacturing process. It goes from the natural sap in a man's own backyard to the finished product on his breakfast table. It is a kind of ancient art, giving a handhold, at least, on the time when individual families and individual communities were virtually self-reliant and well able to survive on their own.

A number of us find ourselves thinking these days in terms of survival. We wonder whether, in this imperiled world, we may one day be forced to fall back on our own resources. Conceivably this small and closely knit country town could make it on its own. We even have a museum with a large collection of tools from the days when this was a do-it-yourself community. But have we the stamina or enough of the old skills to come close to self-reliance? And does anyone really believe that any town can be an island, free to live on its own?

• • •

Back in 1939, when the town was celebrating its two hundredth birthday, Laura Newton described the way people survived in earlier days:

Each housewife and mother had to get along with what could be raised in field and garden. Home-grown wheat, rye and corn furnished a great deal of the food for the family. A visit to the storeroom, attic and many times the kitchen showed cured hams, shoulders and strips of bacon along with chunks of dried beef hanging from the rafters ready to be cooked for the family's needs. Almost every family had a beef and pork barrel where meat was salted down for future use.

In the corner of the kitchen were the spinning wheels where the mother and girls manufactured woolen yarns for stockings and mittens for the family, as well as finer threads of wool and flax for blankets, table cloths, linsey-woolsey, sheets, blankets, and all manner of clothing for the family. Sheep were raised to produce the wool. A patch of flax furnished the linen. In some of the homes a hand loom was set up and on them many articles were woven. Work was done by the light of "tallow lips" or flickering flame from fireplaces.

Each housewife manufactured her barrel of soft soap stirred with a sassafras stick to make it "come" better, also to give the soap a hint of its perfume. Every scrap of grease was saved even to the intestine skins from all slaughtered animals, over which the lye was poured, secured by leaching water through a barrel packed tightly with wood ashes, and then boiled till it was made into soap, either in the big iron arch kettle or in a brass kettle hanging from the crane of the fireplace.

The candles were all made by pouring tallow into candle molds in which the candle wick had been placed, or by the "dipping process."

There were no sewing machines and most of our ancestors were needle experts. The farmers were sort of Jack-of-all-trades, from raising crops to fitting shoes to their horses and oxen sometimes; and even mending footwear for the family which had probably been made by the traveling shoemaker.

'Twould take a volume to tell of the ability and resourcefulness of those thrifty old pioneers. . . .

* * *

The last Indian on our reservation, a slim and nobly featured man known to his tribe as "Running Deer," has died at age 72. He was not a full-blooded Schaghticoke, but he had spent the greater part of his life in our town, and he could trace his lineage back to Eunice Mauwee, "the Christian Indian Princess." (And because there were Jeromes among his ancestors, he was sure of his relation to Lady Randolph Spencer-Churchill, or "Jennie," the Brooklyn-born daughter of the nineteenth-century millionaire Leonard Jerome, and the mother of Sir Winston Churchill.) He is best remembered for his knowledge of the rattlesnakes that inhabit the dens on the mountain behind the reservation. He would catch them alive and ship them off to the Bronx Zoo. The remaining rattlesnakes can rest easy. The reservation stands empty.

* * *

Now it's official. We will lose what is left of our passenger train service on May 1. Only the daily freight will come through, and perhaps only for a while. The federal government, through Amtrak, the National Railway Passenger Corporation, is going to try to rejuvenate a skeletal selection of the nation's passenger routes, but we are not included. Ironically, the industrialist who owned this house before us, using it as a weekend and summer place, and who argued for the preservation of the infrequent local trains, is to be appointed the first head of Amtrak.

* * *

The other day, describing the peculiarities of her large and mostly rural 47-town district, our congresswoman said, "This is where you can't get anywhere from any place."

•   •   •

"The truth is, our railroad way of life came to an end years ago when we stopped getting the traveling salesmen who would come to town by train and stay overnight at the little inns. What we are hearing now is just the death rattle. I think it was a friendlier, easier-going town in those days. We'd sit around on the lawns and porches of Main Street, visiting with each other, far into the night. If you wanted a fishing license after midnight you could get it at the general store. But all that was long ago."

•   •   •

"These things only prove that we are not, as they say, an 'un-changing New England town.' We have been changing all the time, perhaps for the better. Not so many years ago, when I was growing up here, most of the kids who started high school didn't stay to graduate. They dropped out and went to work on the farms, or else they left town altogether. Only a few made their life here. If it weren't for the young couples who came to teach at the boarding schools, we would have become an old folks' town, pretty much. But now the young people are staying, more of them than ever. The fact that a couple can marry, practically before they've got a job, and get a loan and build a house with all sorts of appliances—that would have been unimaginable in former days. If they married young they'd have to stay with their parents, and they were just stuck for a long time. Now you see these young fellows starting their own little businesses from scratch, right in town. Some families even seem to be building little colonies, putting up their houses near each other. Young people now have so much more in the way of entertainment than even the most wealthy people used to have, especially tele-vision and the convenience of going anywhere in your own car.

You can get to the big stores easily. The result is that people aren't so city-minded anymore. They feel they have as much here as they could get in the city."

• • •

In the city, guests at a dinner party sometimes bring flowers. Here we have people who bring us little trees in large pots.

• • •

Some late-winter news items:

— After a long search, someone has finally been found who is willing to serve the town as civil defense director.

— The chamber of commerce plans to have an identification sign painted and mounted on the covered bridge, nearly two centuries after Jacob Bull put it up, so that the tourists who stop to photograph it will know its name.

— The early word is that the town budget will rise for the coming fiscal year from $770,000 to $816,000. Local taxes will increase nine percent.

— The nursery school is looking for a new teacher. Open to children of all faiths, it began in the Episcopal parish house a few years ago, and it has already, like the volunteer FISH organization, made itself indispensable in the life of the town.

— A "Little Theater" is being organized by a local group.

— Four youngsters, eight and nine years old, slipped into the Center School Sunday afternoon, turned on the water taps, tossed around paintpots and redecorated chairs with glue and thumbtacks. But they were caught in the act by the principal. Police and parents were called to the scene. "One mother fainted when she saw the damage," the regional paper reports, "and the doctor was summoned to revive her."

— The Future Planning Committee of the Congregational church, endeavoring to "meet the needs of the youth in the community," has managed to inspire a number of the town's teenagers to organize a youth center and work up a regular program of activities: coffee-hour discussions, poetry readings, film and music shows. They have chosen the name "Inspiration Shack." When one boy protested that "we can't call it 'Inspiration'— that's too religious," a friend replied, "Sure we can: religion is *in.*"

— The town's new citizens' environmental organization is arranging with the selectmen for facilities at the dump for the recycling of glass, paper and tires. "Let this community become a model in the practice of ecological thrift," says the local weekly. "Anything we can do to extend the usefulness of this planet for supporting life is laudable."

• • •

People here worry a lot about the planet these days, and about this unspoiled country area, and about the future of the town. A French couple, writing in the *Reader's Digest* after touring the United States, speak of their surprise that "the America of yesteryear [is] still so easy to find, with white clapboard houses and verandas, with squirreled lawns, church suppers and Sunday schools, quiet lives." An old friend of ours, Ralph Graves, now the managing editor of *Life*, decided after his own tour of the nation that "this country, for all its current disharmony and protest and shouting, is inhabited by people who prefer to be decent to one another."

It is all true, just as it is true that fully two thirds of this small and densely populated state in the crowded Northeast is still green forest—but for how long? What changes are coming? What changes should we welcome? What can we, or should we, avoid? Do we know what kind of future we want, and are we willing to sacrifice for it? And will we, as we work to preserve what we believe to be the best things in life, turn inward and selfish and hostile to the like aspirations of our fellowmen?

• • •

A man's health requires as many acres of meadow to his prospect as his farm does loads of muck. These are the strong meats on which he feeds. A town is saved, not more by the righteous men in it than by the woods and swamps that surround it.

                                        HENRY DAVID THOREAU

*   *   *

"I don't think we're going to have a lot of industrial development or even big housing projects. We're just not geographically suited for it. What we have is natural zoning. There are too many hills to put a good-sized acreage together, and most landowners are determined to hold on to their land. Over the years, I suppose, we'll just take in more and more people and end up as a residential, suburban-type thing—a bedroom town for a bigger town, full of commuters."

*   *   *

"In the old days, the selectmen and the other town fathers were farmers, most of them, and they had almost a do-nothing attitude. They didn't want industry, and they didn't want to do anything that cost money. It was not their idea to put the town on the map: that would only stir things up and bring in a lot of undesirables. But now we know that we can't just sit still and hope for the best. If you want the town to develop in a certain direction, then you've got to work at it."

*   *   *

"There's one man here whose ancestors go way back in this particular area. He has a beautiful hunk of land of about 100 acres or so that he's been holding on to: the old farm where the family started out. He's one of those who's for keeping people out. If you hear him talking on the street to an old neighbor, he says we've got to keep this place nice and quiet; that sort of thing. But I went walking through his land with him one day, and he admitted, 'When the time comes and the price is right, I'll sell.' I just wonder how many more people are thinking the same way."

*   *   *

If you ask us, the people of the small towns of this area may be able to buy time if they can band together. . . . We don't know how much time can be bought—and we're not precisely clear what it is we are seeking to avoid. Connecticut—ALL of Connecticut—is in Megalopolis, a complex of cities and suburbs extending from Portland, Maine, to Richmond, Virginia. The trick is to learn to live with this, not avoid it.

The Good Times Dispatch

•   •   •

"What I hate to see is people moving into town because they want to get away from all these dangers, and then as soon as they're in they don't want to let anyone else in. Shut the door! Raise the drawbridge! And they go around warning about the terrible things that will happen to the town if we don't do so and so. Well, the farmers and others who have been here all their lives, they don't have the same sense of urgency. They're used to gradual change, and since they don't see the dangers, they don't want the restrictions. Maybe they're wrong. Maybe there is an avalanche coming. But you don't change people's way of thinking overnight."

•   •   •

"I agree wholeheartedly," writes a local teacher, "that this way of life need not vanish if we really care enough about the quality and character of our towns and cities. But, man, don't you realize that this means some kind of master planning for whole regions? It means environmental design on a large scale. But more, it means environmental *control*, because on a short term, anyway, quality life is not profitable. And profits—repeat, *profits*—are what America was built on."

•   •   •

Suddenly we have to worry about regionalization. This and neighboring towns learned a while ago that the State Planning

Office had drawn new lines on the map and lumped us in with several large urban and suburban communities in a projected regional planning district. Shocked into action, our various selectmen sounded out public opinion and protested that we were low-population, low-industry country towns who preferred to stick together in our own group. Just by saying that, however, and getting the state to agree, we have taken a long and unintentioned stride toward regionalization.

There are 13 regional planning districts now functioning in the state, taking in 140 of the 169 towns, and some of them have been busy for ten and more years devising and carrying out regional plans, cooperating on open-space preservation and other land use, developing common medical and other public institutions and creating intertown facilities and services.

Even though there is no visible loss of a town's special identity, and the price of cooperation is not high, the little hill towns along this river valley have either ignored or actively resisted the whole idea. And this despite their more than 30 years of sharing a common high school. Cost is one reason, even though a regional planning agency qualifies for state and federal matching grants. Now, like it or not, the case for regionalization becomes increasingly persuasive. A pooling of talents and resources seems not only inevitable but desirable. After all, special-interest outsiders are already planning our future: power companies, highway engineers, land developers, business interests. We might as well have a hand in it, too.

•   •   •

A selection of recent headlines from newspapers and magazines:

COUNTDOWN FOR SMALL TOWNS

INTERSTATE HIGHWAYS: LIFE CHANGES IN THEIR PATHS

NEW ENGLANDERS BUCK TREND TOWARD BULLDOZER

We Can Save Our Towns

Plunder of the Countryside Must Be Halted

Life in the City Sends Some Back to the Farm

Exodus Goes On from Cities to Suburbs

Many States and Cities Putting Brakes on Growth

Economic Growth: New Doubts About an Old Ideal

Small Towns Left Isolated as Airlines Cut Service

Thousands Flee the Towns of America's Lonely Plains

Is Main Street Still There?

• • •

On this mournful and drizzly Sunday afternoon several families form a caravan in their lined-up station wagons. We drive to Dog Tail Corners on the other side of Mount Algo. From there we go in procession far up a twisting and heaving mountain road until it disappears at the ruins of an old schoolhouse. Then, after making sure that the doctor has brought along his snake-bite kit, we hike on muddy trails to a ghost village. An abandoned graveyard, a broken-down mill, crumbling stone walls and a hundred dank and weedy cellar holes testify to the nineteenth-century time when this was a thriving little community.

• • •

You can find these ghost villages all over New England: settlements that died off because their natural resources gave out or economic change made them obsolete or hard times struck a crippling blow. A smallpox epidemic in the 1890s wiped out Woodinville on Ore Hill, just across the river. The ironworkers' settlement at the foot of Skiff Mountain disappeared with our iron industry. For that matter, the once distinctive school districts and postal districts in this town, each with its own shops and one-man industries, faded away with the centralization of the town's business and service activities.

In our own small way, like a model in a wind tunnel, we reveal some of America's contradictory forces—the consolidating and diversifying forces—which are shifting people from one part of the country to another and draining the life out of some places while swamping others. Somehow, as rural people drift to the cities and city people flee to the suburbs, as the countryside empties here and fills up there, we seem to survive and thrive. But not so other good towns, especially those deep in the heartland and the far reaches of the Great Plains. The farm-to-city movement of tens of millions of rural people has withered hundreds of towns that once were bustling with activity and bursting with pride. It remains to be seen whether the whole way of life they represent is going for good.

· · ·

Now they are saying the inland towns are dying, that the prairie towns are giving way to the coyote's call, the railroad's rumble, and the vast strips of cities we call urban sprawls corrode the landscape.

I say rubbish!

Perhaps the people are pouring into the cities, but I believe time will see a reversal of this trend—and a revival of small-town Americana.

This renaissance will not come about until the people of this country drop their benighted idea that the cities possess the good of the country—that they somehow represent in their homes, businesses and life styles the epitome of American civilization.

LARRY VAN GOETHEM, CITY EDITOR
The Janesville Gazette, WISCONSIN

· · ·

Does it matter to us in this fortunate country town that things are going badly for other towns in far places? And for city neighborhoods too? Should we care about the fate of Concord, New Hampshire, and Sugar Loaf, New York? Or Salmon, Idaho, and Steamboat Springs, Colorado? Or Chadds Ford, Pennsylvania, and Sleepy Eye, Minnesota? And what of Newark and Detroit, or Harlem and Watts? Or Bogotá, Calcutta and Saigon?

To my own children, at least, and to others of their generation, the questions need hardly be asked, because the answers are only too obvious. As I write this, Jan is on a kibbutz by the Sea of Galilee, cutting bananas at five in the morning. Eric is writing to an Ethiopian student who will come here next summer to live with us for a year. Julie and Carol are as aware of the stunted and brutish life of the greater part of mankind as they are sensitive to the most fragile flower in the field.

These children, and perhaps yours too, are natives of the global village; nothing and no one that lives is alien to them. They hear that people are in flight from the problems that beset them, escaping if they can to the woods. But they live by the woods, and they know there is no escape from problems and responsibilities, nor should there be.

When old Peter Skiff went up for his first airplane ride on his 100th birthday, he came down complaining that he had been able to see only the town and not the whole earth. Our children live in the age when man has touched the moon and probed the planets. They see the world round and small and precious, to be handled with care.

They should know, as they move toward maturity, that concern for the good earth and caring for the human family is not special to their generation alone. It is something that bridges the boundary lines of age; the generations can sustain and teach each other.

Our children should know that two decades ago their parents sat as a young married couple at a commencement exercise in the Harvard Yard and heard the author of *Our Town,* still young at

54, speak of the way the twentieth century is "shifting its foundations and altering its emphases with striking rapidity." The experts then were calling it the "Age of Upheaval" and the "Age of Anxiety," and the graduating seniors, who were 12 years old at the time of Pearl Harbor, had spent their lives in stormy or threatening weather without ever knowing "that evenly-running world to which one of our Presidents gave the name of Normalcy."

In the 1920s, Thornton Wilder continued, "we used to talk of our expectation of happiness. You can't imagine how seldom you hear the word 'happiness' today, except colored by derision, but with this has come a whole shift in the concept of responsibility." Young people of the new age have "shown me over and over again that to them it is as simple as breathing that all societies are but variants of one another, that somehow all wars from now on are civil wars, and the human adventure is much the same in all times and all places. . . .

"It is disturbing to have lost the feeling of belonging to one reassuring community, to New England or the United States, or to Western civilization, to be sustained and supported by one of these localizations. But they are gone, they are going, and they are gone in that sense of being a psychic nest. . . .

"Oh, it is a lonely and alarming business to feel one's self one in the creation of billions and billions, and especially if your parents seem never to have felt that sensation at all, but it is exciting and inspiriting to be among the first to hail and accept the only fraternal community that finally can be valid—that emerging, painfully emerging unity of those who live on the one inhabited star."

· · ·

Now the long winter is over. Spring slipped in this evening at three minutes to eight. It is the 232nd spring in the history of our town. We can feel the earth stirring, hear creatures announcing the new season, see hope in the ripening buds of the dogwoods.

The wintering birds, arguing over the sunflower seeds we have scattered on the melting sheet of snow, have been joined by a robin. We are moved by these signs of renewal and by the prospect of witnessing once again on this mountaintop the glory of the earth reborn.

We dare to speak the word "happiness."